CHOSEN

Principles for Achieving your DESTINY

Cheryl Nelson, M.Ed.

© Copyright 2017

All rights reserved

Printed in the United States of America.

ISBN: 978-0-692-99919-6

THANKS & ACKNOWLEGEMENTS

I would like to thank my Mother, Mary Nelson for all the many sacrifices she made in her life to ensure her children would have a better life. Also, for her words of wisdom that she has imparted into her children lives that still resonates in my mind and keeps me reaching for greatness.

I would like to thank and acknowledge the Reviewers of this book and my prayer partners who encouraged me to "go for it" when I became discouraged and couldn't see the completion of this book with my natural eyes.

And lastly, I would like to acknowledge the next generation and all my nieces & nephews to press towards the goal to win the prize for which God has called you heavenward in Christ Jesus.

Contents

Acknowledgements

Preface III

Introduction 1

Chapter 1: The Principle of Discipline 20
A Soldier's Life of Discipline
The Fiery Furnace
Discipline Activity
Review points of Discipline

Chapter 2: The Principle of Perseverance ... 36
Unavoidable obstacle
The Persistent Widow
A grain of mustard seed
When the enemy comes in like a flood
Life's Goals Activity
Review points of Perseverance

Chapter 3: The Principle of Prayer 57
Instrumental Bible Characters
Connecting Tracks
Train up a Child
Prayer of Salvation
Review points of Prayer

Chapter 4: The Principle of Faith 81
Predestined
Prayer & Faith
Cheryl Miraculous Healing

Fear of the unknown
John Smith Story
Your Testimony
Review points of Faith

Chapter 5: The Principle of Humility 105
Jesus's Birth
Characters of Jesus
Doe's Family Dynamics
Humility Activity
Review points of Humility

Chapter 6: The Principle of Serving 125
Servanthood Characteristics
Jesus being a Servant
Serving in Ministry
Servanthood Activity
Review points of Serving

Chapter 7: The Principle of Identity 136
The Road to Damascus
Bible Characters Identity
Defining your Identity
The Prodigal Son
Guard & Protect your Identity
Sunday School Trivia
Reflections Activity
Review points of Identity

Personal Reviews 160
About the Author 164
Footnotes / References / Websites 167
Copyright / Permission / Credits 169
Scriptures References 172

Preface

Chosen came into focus whereby a few realities: I wanted to ensure those coming after me won't waste any more time and energies on those things that are not important or beneficial to obtaining what God has purposed for you to have, and/ or pertaining to your DESTINY.

In every course of life or scholastic endeavor you desire to pursue, there are basic fundamentals to understand in order to achieve your goals. Start out building on a firm foundation first and you will be able to meet your objectives successfully.

When we are faced with challenges and obstacles, we fail to realize that there's always another way to get what you are aiming for. The 7 principles and activities were designed as handy tools to help you remain focused and motivated to get the things you were destined to achieve. The scripture references throughout the book will help strengthen your faith while you search the scriptures during your reading session/s. You will be able to complete the whole book in the first setting; I'm confident you will find something helpful to your current situation.

The devil is not your problem. The enemy will and can cause great problems for you, but remember he is already defeated! The devil can not take what belong to you, unless you let him/her have it. You already have the power to be successful and get what's yours. And don't let anyone tell you any different for what you know belong to you; you are the head and not the tail!

Introduction

It was many years ago now when I lived in Columbia, SC during my mid-twenties. A few years after moving to Columbia, I rededicated my life back to Christ. I had received Christ around the age of 15 years old during a week revival at my home church in Bonneau, SC. Back then when I was growing up as a teenager, we had to, "seek & tarry" a whole week, to become a born again child of God, L.O.L. Some people and/or the new millennials haven't heard of that term before -- if you're not from the ole-school. But several years had passed and I had stumbled a few times trying to hold on to my faith and living the Christian life as a young adult.

I moved from the small town of Bonneau to the capital city of Columbia, SC in pursuit of completing my education and becoming an independent woman.
After high school, I worked a few years at a factory as an assembly worker; that job eventually ended. I knew I wanted to do

something productive with my life. I was also engaged when I left home to a young man I thought would be my future husband. It didn't work out, and we eventually went our separate ways. From what I gathered as we parted, it appeared that I was becoming too independent as I was trying to find my way. We tried to keep the relationship intact, but we had separate agendas and we just could not find our happy medium.

One evening after class, I returned home and opened the door to find the things he had given me were gone. He had given me those things for my 1st new apartment. Of course, I had some choice words for him!

While in Columbia, I joined a Baptist church in the area where I lived. My family had driven to Columbia that Sunday morning from Bonneau, SC for my baptism.

As I look back on those days, I saw my life literally changing right before my eyes. I was leaving the carnal way of living and thinking and becoming a young lady on the righteous *chosen* path.

Introduction

One of the ladies I worked with asked me to attend church with her one Sunday. She was a great person with a humble spirit. She was always smiling and I had never seen her wear pants (I didn't think anything of it, I knew she loved God). She asked me several times to go to church with her, so I eventually decided to go. I decided on the perfect Sunday that I would go with her since I didn't have to serve at my church that Sunday.

We met early that Sunday morning for her church service; one of her son's was on the drums. As I looked around the sanctuary, I felt out of place. All the ladies were wearing a much longer skirt or dress than the dress I was wearing. And to my surprise, **NO-ONE** was wearing makeup, but me.

I felt embarrassed, and wondered if I should slip out without anyone noticing me. By the end of the service, everyone was assembled in a prayer circle. I tried not to make eye contact with anyone. Then the pastor had called me out (I was very nervous, I thought he was about to rebuke me and tell me not to come back). He began to give me what I know now to be a word of prophesy.

Even though I felt out of place there, I was accepted by God that day, as he delivered a special word to me.

My girlfriend and I talked about what the pastor had imparted to me, and we kept looking forward to the manifestation.

I continued growing and serving on the usher's ministry in the church where I was baptized until I started attending a prayer group with some other friends. I told a few of my friends and co-workers that I was feeling like it was time for me to move on from where I had been serving for maybe 5 or 6 years now.

I finally went to my pastor to talk with him about leaving. He gave me his blessings and I will forever be grateful for Pastor James Abrams who baptized me, and got me back on the righteous *chosen* path.

One of the churches in the nearby area was pretty popular and I attended one of their

Introduction

Sunday evening services. I was so moved by the sermon that was preached to the point the message was life changing for me. I experienced unstoppable tears. The pastor had spoken as if God told him that I was in the service that evening -- he read my mail!

The pastor shared a word on the life of a human being whose life was shaped and *chosen* by God. The message had gotten in my spirit and I kept holding on to what he said about being *chosen* (a royal priesthood, a holy nation, set apart, picked by God). I accepted that the pastor was talking to me, and I was also *chosen,* I believe now, from a small child.

Sometime later I got a personalized license plate designed with the word, *"chosen."* I still have that license plate until this day. I really didn't know spiritually what was happening then, but I knew in my soul I was *chosen*. The word became me, to the point a few of my close friends started calling me *chosen*. I didn't know it then that my first book would be entitled, **"CHOSEN!"**

CHOSEN

> *But you are a chosen generation, a royal priesthood, a holy nation. His own special people that you may proclaim the praises of Him who called you out of darkness into His marvelous light (I Peter 2:9), nkjv.*

I was working a full time job at the Department of Transportation where I made many friends and associates; I resigned that position after six years. Later I started a part time job about the last 6 to 8 months before the move to Georgia in order to finish my education. I continued growing in the Word and God's grace as I had joined the prayer ministry, and I was a faithful member in several other ministries.

The summers were especially a lot of fun because many young adults like me attended and helped with Vacation Bible School. Not only were there fun games but we played bible drills and I became very competitive at winning. I always looked forward to finding the most bible scriptures, during the bible drills. At the end of the evening the winners would get a special prize. I accumulated lots of them.

Introduction

The church I joined held several events for the Singles Ministry. Once I was even asked to give the prayer for one of our events.... That was a big deal for me because I knew how to pray, but whenever someone would ask me to pray in public, I would feel anxious, nervous and afraid. But I got through it and everyone thought I did a good job.

Other friends and several singles from the neighborhood churches were invited to travel with our Singles Ministry to Cedine Ministries in Spring City, Tennessee a few times. It was exciting to meet other singles from several other states as we all had one thing in common, we were single and on a righteous path.

Betty and I would always encourage each other to attend the Single's Retreat in Tennessee since we had been friends for several years; we decided to be roommates and scope out the single male counterparts.
We would be up for most of the night just talking, laughing and having fun with the other singles in the house. We took lots of

pictures and enjoyed the outdoors nature scenes of Cedine.

During this time there were many friends and associates that would come to me regarding choices and decisions they were struggling with in their lives. As young adults, we all shared some of the same concerns. Some were struggling with identity issues, dating and trying to maintain a Christian life to please God were always at the top of the list.

Other concerns were college choices and applying for student loans, finding employment or a roommate to help with expenses.

I would share my experiences and speak with them about their future goals, making wise choices and allowing the Lord to be a part of their lives. I even invited them to attend my church and prayer night. Now I can understand how I ventured into Psychology for my undergraduate degree. Before I started working in this profession, I was already doing the work for free.

Introduction

I eventually completed the two years Associate of Science Degree at a local technical college in Columbia, SC. I was a few years older than many of my classmates and I wasn't sure what was next, but I knew there was more to come. I worked several years after high school, and later decided that I needed to pursue my education ….. in something.

One of my high school friends lived in Atlanta and I went to visit with her on several occasions; I thought how wonderful it would be to move to Georgia! They called it, "Hotlanta," during that time. There was always stuff to do when I visited with friends who lived there. I was telling my friends in Columbia that Atlanta is the place to be!

I had only visited a few other states during that time so, to move to Georgia, would be just grand, coming from the small town of Bonneau.

My friends and prayer partners were excited for me but some of them were also upset with me because I was moving. I didn't allow any distractions to stop my progress, and I kept it moving. I would miss them also but I was feeling like there was much more for me to accomplish. The male friends I had were not talking about anything long term so I didn't have the worry of leaving someone behind.

Two of the young men I worked with at UPS helped me pack up my one bedroom apartment in a small U-Haul, and I was off to Atlanta, G-e-o-r-g-i-a!

I later found out that the young girl who lived a few doors down from my apartment had also left for Atlanta shortly after I left.

I didn't have a job when I moved to Georgia, but I went right over to UPS and told them I worked for their location in Columbia, SC part time. That helped me get the job with UPS in Atlanta!

My home-girl allowed me to stay with her family until I got my own place a few months later.

Shortly thereafter I was admitted to Georgia State University to complete my Bachelor Degree in Psychology. I knew God was helping me because I had appealed the school's

Introduction

decision that would not allow me to enroll as a Georgia resident. Instead, the school wanted me to pay the out-of-state tuition fees. I had already established myself as a resident of Georgia.

I had a job and had recently gotten my own apartment. It was truly a blessing when Georgia State granted my appeal and reversed their previous decision in my favor.

Remember, don't stop at the first "no" there's always a blessing following.

I had contemplated and procrastinated for a few years after moving to Georgia about starting a non-profit business. I later relocated to Boston, MA where I worked as an admissions recruiter.

While recruiting prospectus students, I met several women who I envisioned would be prefect candidates for the program I wanted to launch. I had done most of the foundational work to naming the business and making the annual fees, but I never did anything with it.

CHOSEN

Every prophesy I heard was all telling me the same thing about helping women and starting a business but I kept stalling.

I didn't feel as if I was experienced enough to start the business and I couldn't find anyone who was doing this kind of work. I had so many questions but no answers.

Several years ago after relocating back to GA; I wasn't accustomed to that type of cold weather in Boston, being from the south. My dad also became ill while I was living there and attending graduate school. It was difficult going back-n-forth from Boston to SC to see him. After graduation I couldn't wait to return to Georgia where it is much warmer and closer to SC.

I was minding my own business one afternoon when I stopped at a service station in the Metro Atlanta area --- that I was not familiar with to get some gas. A gentleman rolled up on me and asked me, could he finish pumping my gas.

I didn't even see the direction he came from, but all of a sudden, he just appeared, it happened so fast.

Introduction

I couldn't tell you what kind of car he was driving since I didn't see one.

I didn't know this man from Adam and he didn't know me. The man started telling me those things I was hearing from previous prophesies. I had never met him before, but after exchanging just a few words of greetings with him, he started prophesying to me right there at the gas pump.
I said, "WOW," I looked dumbfounded. I later found out that the man worked in the ministry at his church. God made it so that I kept hearing the same thing -- even from strangers.

One night as I was reading before bed, I picked up my pen and pad to write down a few things I thought would inspire my young adult nieces and nephews to avoid some of the pitfalls and mistakes I made on my Christian journey. I thought I had experienced everything that life could offer by this time, and I didn't want them to make the same mistakes I made and also for them to be watchful of the devil!

When we were growing up and someone would mention the word "devil," as young children, we would think that the devil wore a red tight spandex suit with black horns carrying a black pitchfork.

You will hear several names that the devil is called --- the evil one, satan, the tempter, adversary, lucifer, the accuser, an evil spirit, etc.

If you are not watchful and prayerful, the devil can easily try to force you or trick you to be a part of his or her team. The devil is very cunning at his/ her disguises. Even adults and seasoned saints are being tricked and bamboozled out of their identity because they have hung out with the devil too long.

NEVER .... give the devil a ride, soon he will try to drive.

Introduction

And no wonder, since satan himself masquerades as an angel of light. So it is no great surprise if his servants also masquerade as servants of righteousness, but their end will correspond with their deeds (II Corint. 11:14-15), amp.

That night I started writing, and writing, and writing, and before you know it, I had completed the introduction and about four chapters of this book. It was flowing so easy until it felt as if I was on to something.

I shut my Bible, put the pen down and went to bed, but my spirit did not stop. I kept hearing more revelation, like the whole book was being downloaded into my spirit. It was about 3:00 AM, and I was tired; but I was disappointed I could not keep up with the spirit.

I have about twenty nieces and nephews ranging in age from young girls and boys, to teenagers, some young adults, and there are also a few grown ones.

CHOSEN

I had already seen some of them make some very costly mistakes ---- like I did, and I wanted to impart some wisdom to them. I also thought that this would be a great opportunity to share with likeminded ordinary folks who could benefit from my experiences and embrace freedom and wisdom.

I had shared my notes of this book with a girlfriend and prayer partner. She and I had been friends for more than twenty years. She and I had prayed many, many prayers and seen God changed things. We both have seen prayers answered instantly, we've seen a few days passed before prayers were answered, and sometimes we just had to wait a while before the prayers were answered. But our prayers were always answered.

That night I wrote down four titles that were flowing as I continued to be amazed at what was happening with this book. I shared the four titles with my girlfriend that I contemplated for my book. When I mentioned, **"Chosen,"** my

Introduction

friend said, "Cheryl, I believe that's it because you already had that name a long time ago." O.M.G!!! My friend had picked up the same revelation I was sensing in my spirit. I started praying for a sign and confirmation, out of the mouth of two or three witnesses let my word be established (II Corint. 13:1). I prayed specifically that it would be the voice of significant influences in my life. So, that's when *"CHOSEN"* was rebirthed. One confirmation came from Pastor Bishop Eddie Long the following Sunday after I prayed for a confirmation. Bishop Long stood up there preaching some of the things that were written in this book.

My mouth fell open in amazement! His was the first voice of significant influence. The other voice was one of the Elders at New Birth who led and trained the prayer team ministry that I had joined years ago, before moving to Boston.

This confirmation came to me by text message, "you were *chosen* to be the leader on the bus to Stone Mountain." Elder Jerry Wilson was the second voice of significant influence.

CHOSEN

After those two confirmations, I kept hearing this title from many other people. I said …. I know this is it!

I didn't know then more than twenty years ago when I got the name, *"chosen"* in a Sunday evening service, it would have to go through the birthing process until now …… the fulfillment.

For you are a people holy to the Lord your God. The Lord your God has chosen you out of all the peoples on the face of the earth to be His people, His treasured possession (Deut. 7:6), niv.

Introduction

My former Pastor, Bishop Eddie L. Long transitioned to his eternal rest on: Martin Luther King Jr. Birthday on: January 15, 2017.

Chapter 1

The Principle of DISCIPLINE

A Soldier's Life of Discipline

The Fiery Furnace

Discipline Activity

Review

Discipline

But seek aim at and strive after, first of all his kingdom and his righteous (His way of doing and being right) and then all of these things taken together will be given you (Matt. 6:33), amp.

"The practice of training people to obey rules or a code of behavior, using punishment to correct disobedience; training that corrects, molds or perfects the mental faculties or moral character, self-control," (Dictionary.com/ Merriam-Webster.com).

Discipline is one of those tough words that some people choose to remove from their vocabulary or even their life. Discipline is not always easy or simple to achieve in one's life but it is one of the main ingredients for greatness and reaching your destiny. If you have incorporated discipline in your life, then you have what it takes to become successful in every area of your life, and you will be able to overcome any form of adversity brought by the enemy.

CHOSEN

Otherwise, if you are not embracing a life of discipline then you won't have the strength or stamina to fight the many giants that will show up in your life.

Many times we don't go out looking for the devil; since you have the character of Jesus, you desire to be peaceful in all things. But there will be times when adversity will just show up when you least expect it.

A disciplined life causes you to remain focused and fixed on spiritual things to fight the devil with spiritual weapons, not carnal weapons which will not bring us victory.

Remember, you have already won this fight, it doesn't matter which battle you're in. You haven't won by what you "see" in front of you, or by what you are experiencing right now; you have only won this battle by trusting God's plan for you, and by your FAITH.

The Principle of Discipline

Every scripture is God breathed and profitable for instruction, for reproof and conviction of sin, for correction of error and discipline in obedience for training in righteousness (in holy living, in conformity to God's will in thought, purpose, and action). So that the man of God may be complete and proficient, well fitted and thoroughly equipped for every good work (II Tim. 3:16-17), amp.

When you maintain a fervent prayer life, study the Word to show yourself approve, attend church and bible study regularly and don't forget to submit yourself to God and resist the devil, this has afforded you to embrace a disciplined life on the righteous path.

A Soldier's Life of discipline

When you think of the career of a soldier (army, navy, marines) the military career gives me an overall good picture of someone having a disciplined life.

CHOSEN

From what I've learned from family members and friends who have careers in the military, they would say, "it's very difficult for the first 6 months to a year."

The soldier must understand and accept that if he/she wants to be successful or advance in ranks, then he must maintain a high quality of discipline. The soldier will endure physical, emotional and psychological stressors on various levels. If the soldier chooses to accept a leadership or staff sergeant position, then not only does the soldier have to endure a high level of discipline for himself, but he/she will also have the responsibility to make sure that everyone else in the unit is disciplined as well.

The term I would like to use here is, **"you got to be on-point."** The soldier will have to make many sacrifices throughout his/her career. The soldier may have to be transferred to a war zone or overseas, then his very life could be at stake to protect and defend his county.

The Principle of Discipline

Let's parallel our lives with that of a soldier in reaching our destiny ….. You can't allow small stuff to distract you, you can't copy what your friends are doing or saying, you have to buckle down and do it God's way. Once you've mastered discipline, then you're on your way to achieving greatness.

Mature Discipline

When you have mastered discipline, you are not afraid to pursue your dreams and goals and you will go after it with all you got; when you have mastered discipline, you will pay your tithes first before going out shopping with your friends; when you have mastered discipline you will be able to encourage someone who may be struggling in an area of their life; when you have mastered discipline you will begin to make wise choices and your life will be fruitful. My point is, when you have mastered discipline you have graduated from grade school and you're now ready to eat meat.

CHOSEN

> *For the commandment is a lamp, and the teaching is light; and reproofs for discipline are the way of life (Prov. 6:23), nasb.*

Evaluate your life right where you are now, does your life yields one of being disciplined? Only you can answer that question. Some of us will choose not to be honest with ourselves; discipline is a very intricate term that's needed in our lives as we strive for greatness and to achieve our destiny.

I learned all about discipline earlier on my journey, after I had rededicated my life back to Christ. I've seen people with a disciplined life and I had also seen the opposite.

I was striving to become more disciplined because I knew from my own personal experiences that you can't ride on every band-wagon.

The Principle of Discipline

There were things in life I wanted to achieve and there were victories to be won as I started to become more Christ-like. God was helping me to put off the old things and strive for the character to be more like Jesus.

Therefore, if anyone is in Christ, he is a new creation. The old has passed away; behold, the new has come (2 Corth. 5:17), nkjv.

Example: If you haven't embraced a disciplined life these are some characteristic you will find: laziness, tale-bearer, follower, drunkard, adulterer, thief, fornicator, gossiper, little faith, etc.

You may have had some problems with becoming more disciplined in your life, or with your time, with your energies or your attention. And you have tried to leave this state of being, but you probably didn't have much success, right? I didn't either.

If you are trying to become more disciplined but using your own efforts or your own will, then you are probably circling the mountain.

Some people refer to this as, "spinning your wheels." You will only get lasting results of a disciplined life, when you use God's plan, the Word and supernatural enforcement.

You will eventually come to grips with the fact that you can not change yourself without the help of God's spirit and the supernatural power of God.

Someone very close to you, your spouse, a best friend, it may have been a family member has told you about your short comings and for you to get your life together and clean up your act. Like the good person that you are, you have told them that you will work on it to straighten out your life.

They didn't really have to tell you because you already know that your life is a total mess. To your surprise, you may have tried to work on everything you could do, to better yourself, from reading self-help books,

The Principle of Discipline

watching videos or even listening to recordings on hypnosis.

You have really tried and tried again to find out that you just keep going back to your same old ways. You've failed again, and again. I will reiterate this point; you can not do it in your own strength; **you will need some super on your natural.**

So you say, "well .... many people have a disciplined and prosperous life without the help of God." Yes, I agree, but I'm not talking about a life that's not submitted to God. The *chosen* life, on the path of righteousness is one that is submitted and is being disciplined daily along the path of holiness. You are not too young, too fabulous, too fine, too old or too beat-up, to understand that you cannot live a successful life without being connected to the vine. God is the true vine ... you ... we are the branches.

If you remain in me and I in you,
you will bear much fruit, Apart from me
you can do nothing (John 15:5), nkjv.

Disciplined into the fiery furnace

In Chapter 3 of Daniel, the three Hebrew Boys are a great example of being disciplined. These young men lived a life of faith and discipline to God. Shadrach, Meshach and Abed-Nego did not compromise their convictions and beliefs to bow down to the golden image (idol) except the true and living God (verse: 14-27).

As a result, the Hebrew Boys were bound and thrown in the fiery furnace, which was set seven times hotter than it was usually heated.

The boys were seen walking around loosed in the furnace and unharmed!! The ropes were the only thing that was burned off the boys. And they didn't even smell like smoke. King Nebuchadnezzar wanted the Hebrew Boys to forget about their God and conform and worship the Babylonian gods.

The Principle of Discipline

Then the king promoted Shadrach, Meshach, and Abednego, in the province of Babylon (v. 30). Oh .... right .... promotions always come with having a disciplined life.

I was actually curious about the boy's ages after I read this story. I thought if those boys were older men, then they may have conformed to the Kings commands. Those boys were young enough to take a stand for what they believed without having others to influence them.

After reading and researching several versions of this story, it was determined that Nebuchadnezzar captured the boys as teenagers and they were taken to Babylon. It was predicted that the three Hebrew Boys were about 20 or 21 years old when they were thrown in the furnace!!

You may have heard many sermons on this story with the three Hebrew Boys, and I have too. After I saw these boy's tenacity and courage it really helped me and grew my faith!

CHOSEN

And your faith will be strengthened also when, "you choose" to trust God and embrace a life of discipline on the *chosen* path. Even though we will have great opposition, He will jump in the fire with us!

***Even though in this life
we will have great oppositions,
God will protect us in the fire!***

I can hardly believe many years ago, I used to curse like a sailor, yep, and other things that may even shock you. I didn't have to ask God to remove cursing from my tongue. It eventually started to fall off when I started reading the Bible, praying and becoming more disciplined.

Here's a sho'nuff trick of the enemy -----
I noticed that some of those things that I'm not proud of now will try to keep a stronghold on you. And if it's not submitted under the power of God, "that thing," of your old nature will try to control you.

The Principle of Discipline

The story of the 3 Hebrews Boys can even help us grown folks, since they were younger than most of us. The Hebrews Boys did not allow "anyone" nor "anything" to change what they believe and their faith in God remain steadfast. They were disciplined at an early age, and God stepped in just as He said he would when you're in trouble (Psa. 50:15).

There are other scriptures that you can reference in the following chapters to help you become more disciplined along the journey in achieving your destiny.

……. no more excuses!

If you live in me (abide vitally united to me) and My words remain in you and continue to live in your hearts, ask whatever you will and it shall be done for you (Jn. 15:5), amp.

CHOSEN

On the lines below, identify area(s) in your life that you may need to be more focused or disciplined.

_____

_____

_____

_____

_____

The Principle of Discipline

<u>*Points to review for the Discipline Principle*</u>

- ✓ *Discipline is needed in the believer's life in order to achieve greatness.*

- ✓ *Discipline is needed to remain focused on spiritual things and becoming mature.*

- ✓ *Having a disciplined life is sometimes not easy to do; you can not achieve discipline in your own strengths.*

- ✓ *Being disciplined helps when you are faced with adversity.*

- ✓ *The chosen path of righteous is one that's disciplined and submitted to the things of God.*

- ✓ *The military soldiers' life parallels with the believer's life with being disciplined.*

- ✓ *You have to stay connected to the true vine in order to maintain a disciplined life.*

- ✓ *The three Hebrew Boys in Daniel 3 are a good example of being submitted and disciplined in achieving greatness.*

Chapter 2

The Principle of PERSEVERANCE

Unavoidable obstacle

The Persistent Widow

A grain of mustard seed

When the enemy comes in like a flood

Life's Goals Activity

Review

Perseverance

Not that I have already attained, or am already perfected; but I press on, that I may lay hold of that for which Christ Jesus has also laid hold of me (Phil: 3:12), nkjv.

"Steadfastness in doing something despite difficulty or delay in achieving success; not giving up," (Dictionary.com / Merriam-Webster.com).

Can you think of a few projects you've started over the years or some life goals that's still on the shelf? Many of us would answer that question with a resounding, Yes!!

You may have experienced some major setbacks or some unavoidable obstacles, but keep pressing forward toward your goal. I cannot begin to tell you the importance of perseverance in reaching your destiny and becoming successful on the righteousness path.

Let's look at some of these obstacles together......

Many of us have experienced more than a few of these obstacles: unexpected pregnancy, car accident, death of a loved one, natural disaster, surgery, termination from a job, life threatening illness, divorce, bankruptcies, house fire, foreclosure, broken relationships, repossessions, law-suits, car died, etc.

These were just to name a few; there are so many other obstacles you can add to this list. I have experienced a few of them myself. But, in the midst of every storm, the sun will shine again (my version).

> *Weeping may endure for a night, but joy cometh in the morning (Psa. 30:5), amp.*

Unavoidable Obstacle

I moved to Atlanta, GA the summer of 1998 in an old Mitsubishi, Mirage, packed with my most valuable possessions and a small U-Haul.

The Principle of Perseverance

That car had more than 300,000 miles on it. I believe it lasted close to 18 years and I was determined to drive it until the wheels rolled off. I wanted and needed a new car but during that time I just couldn't afford a new one, I thought.

I had to go to the mechanic shop several times a month for repairs. I didn't know how I was going to pay for a new car because I was only working a part-time job while I was completing my bachelor's degree at Georgia State University.

I had set out one afternoon on a, "wing & a prayer," to the Honda dealer. I finally made it to the dealership somewhere near Peachtree Dunwoody Road driving only about 50 mph.

I met a salesman there who helped me look around and finally I decided on the car I thought I could afford. I was getting excited that I would eventually return to the dealership to get the car I wanted with the first month's down payment.

CHOSEN

As I was driving back to College Park at Riverdale Road around 9:00pm, my car died right there on I-285! I was trying to make it back home and not paying any attention to the temperature gauge. All-of-a-sudden, I heard, BOOM!! The engine had blown!!

OMG, the engine was smoking!! The smell of antifreeze and smoke filled the car. I didn't have any family or relatives in Georgia that I could call to come get me. There was one friend that I did call, but he never called back.

Directly behind me on the expressway was a nice lady who pulled over when my car went up in smoke. Her name was Joy. She quickly helped me get my things out of the car.
She told me that she was going to meet her husband in College Park for dinner. It was getting late and I didn't want to inconvenience her.

The nice lady said she would drive me home; I wanted to be afraid being new to Atlanta, but the lady made me very comfortable. She took me about 25 to 30 miles to Riverdale Rd, and dropped me off at my apartment complex parking lot. We were talking all the way to my apartment and I was thanking God for her help.

The nice Caucasian lady and I exchanged names and phone numbers. I told her that I wanted to do something nice for her helping me, and driving me home.

I was so frustrated about my car dying; I had to have people help me with rides until I could get another car.

My dad had a friend in SC who was a salesman at a Honda Dealer there. He encouraged me to come home to get a car and he would help me.

I went home a few weeks later to pick out a car that I could afford on a part time job salary.

CHOSEN

The salesman worked out a reasonable payment plan for me, since I was a college student, so, I was driving again! And, I didn't need any money down because the salesmen knew my dad and my dad told him what had happened to my car dying on the interstate.

I returned to GA with a 2-door hunter green, Honda Civic, and I was smiling again. I could not wait to call Joy, the nice lady who had helped me when my car died on I-285.

Joy had only given me one number and I was planning to send her a thank you card. The person on the other end said, "sorry ma'am there's no one here by that name." I asked again in disbelief and checked the number. What!!!

I thought, OMG, who was that, that brought me back to Riverdale, a few weeks ago. Who was this live person? I told everyone about that experience and they all said it was my personal Angel, named Joy (true story)....

The Principle of Perseverance

I'm telling you, there are tangible benefits with being *chosen*. You may not know it right now, but God does!

*You have not **chosen** Me, but I have **chosen** you and I have appointed and placed and purposefully planted you, so that you would go and bear fruit and keep on bearing, and that your fruit will remain and be lasting, so that whatever you ask of the Father in My name He may give to you (John 15:16), amp.*

The Parable of the Persistent Widow:

*There was a judge in a certain city, he said, who neither feared God nor cared about people. A widow of that city came to him repeatedly, saying, give me justice in this dispute with my enemy. The judge ignored her for a while, but finally he said to himself, I don't fear God or care about people, but this woman is driving me crazy. I'm going to see that she gets justice, because she is wearing me out with her constant requests! Then the Lord said, "Learn a lesson from this unjust judge." Even he rendered a just decision in the end. So, don't you think God will surely give justice to his **chosen** people who cry out to him day and night?*

Will he keep putting them off? I tell you, he will grant justice to them quickly! (Luke 18:2-8), nlt.

The parable above is a good example to you and me that you don't have to give up when you don't get a favorable answer the first time. The scripture is intended to show how we should continue to pray and not loose heart. Just as the widow woman was persistent with the unfaithful judge to get justice, we should not give up either on achieving our goals.

If it doesn't happen just like we want it to, when we attempted the first time ---- **don't give up!**

What size is a grain of mustard seed

Some of my sisters (the younger ones), friends and associates refer to these times we're living in as, **"the microwave age."**

The Principle of Perseverance

Everything must be done -- quick, fast and in a hurry. It's amazing to hear their stories of disappointment around the table during heated discussions and debate. No time to wait, no time for patience, lets get it, and do it now.

Oftentimes when we get, **"No"** for an answer we think it's over, and there's no way to move that stubborn mountain from out of your way.

We become discouraged and sad, we give up, we wave the white flag and tell our friends, I'm done. To our surprise if you had enough courage to try it again, this time you have learned something from your previous experiences and you have received wise counsel.

Then when you tried again, you know what you're working with. This time you've added a little more faith than before, and you were able to complete the task at hand.

CHOSEN

That mountain will come down!
Some things just take a little more
time and patience.

The word which came to Jeremiah from the Lord, saying; Arise and go down to the potter's house, and there I will cause you to hear My words. Then I went down to the potter's house, and there He was, making something at the wheel. And the vessel that He made of clay was marred in the hand of the potter; so He made it again into another vessel, as it seemed good to the potter to make (Jere. 18:1-4), nkjv.

Since you have already been *chosen* by The Most High God to have a great destiny, it's okay when you don't ace the first test, the cake didn't turn out right, or you've failed Physics. You will always have another opportunity to try it again, until you get it just the way you want it. Stay on the path of righteousness, you too are *chosen*.

The Principle of Perseverance

*Let us not become weary in doing good,
for at the proper time we will reap a harvest
if we do not give up (Gal. 6:9), niv.*

When the enemy comes in like a flood

As I was completing the final contents of this book, I was reminded of the **"hard warfare"** I came through over the previous year, but Jesus kept me! I believe had I stayed the path when I started writing this book during the spring of 2016, it could have been published by the beginning of 2017.

I told my reviewers that I would get a rough draft to them several months ago then, but that time came and past and I became discouraged that I had put the book down because of all I had to endure.

I had become discouraged for a season, and sometimes you will also. Now I know that when you step out to believe God, the enemy pulls out his "big-guns" to stop you.

CHOSEN

I had prayed and asked God for a sign and confirmation for the title of this book and I got it. Not only from the two people I mentioned in the introduction but every time I turned around someone was telling me about this title, *"chosen,"* or a situation that I had already written in one of these seven chapters.

It appeared that I was hearing the word *chosen* much more frequently now... It was amazing to see what God was doing. All I had to do was to be obedient and stay focused.
God will make it plain for you to see what He wants you to do. Then, I knew this book would be a blessing to many.

"See, what had happened was"...... when you hear or see those five words together, LOOK-OUT, you know the devil is lurking around somewhere. The enemy was using people against me that I really cared about (family, coworkers and close acquaintances).

The Principle of Perseverance

As I think about it now, I just couldn't believe it (no one is exempt from the attacks of the enemy). It was very obvious these people had turned on me and tried to make things very difficult for me. When you find yourself getting into hostile verbal disputes and arguments almost to becoming physical (this has never been my character), you know someone is being used by the devil (II Corint. 10:4).

You will know these acts are straight from the devil because they really don't make any sense, petty, vicious, mockery and downright not necessary.

I would like to think that I'm a peaceable person, easy going and friendly. On my resume where you list personal strengths, one of mine is, "strong work ethics."

CHOSEN

This comes from how we were raised growing up. We were taught at home to do what you're supposed to do, on those people job. I can see this trait in all of my siblings also.

My work bares my name so I would like to make sure I'm working as unto the Lord. My character and integrity speaks of who I am as a God fearing woman. That's no secret. You will know without a doubt, only the devil would be mad about what God is doing in someone's life. God wants to bless you; and the devil is fighting to destroy you.

This will help you ---- if you have been attacked by someone you love, trust, worked with or even prayed with; they may even be of the faith, or having strong faith you may say. **Don't. Take. A. Second. Thought.**

Many times they don't know they are being used by an evil spirit. The light in you is provoking the darkness in them to come in alignment with the true spirit of God, and this is why you and I are attacked.

The Principle of Perseverance

If you try to make some sense out of all the hostility, deception and contention that's coming against you, don't be disappointed when you don't get the answers you're seeking. They won't acknowledge or even remember attacking you, (this situation can easily be turned against you to make you look like the culprit or the one who started all of this confusion). Be prayerful and very careful during this season.

You just have to accept the fact that the devil doesn't like you because you are *chosen* and you look like and talk like the person who defeated him and sent him to hell. You are serious about your faith and you reverence the True and Living God. You don't have to make excuses that you love God. In cases like these, I will remind you to **stay focused and trust God, this isn't your fight** (II Chron. 20:16 & 17).

Think about the term "deception" just for a brief moment. Deception can be seen in its highest form and its where most of our attacks originates. We know all about deception very well at the beginning of creation and also throughout the Bible. Deception has wrought great havoc for many of the Bible Characters and it's still here lurking in the world today. If you are not walking in the truth or discerning the influences of the evil one, then you too can easily be deceived.

Deception is very subtle (**you won't be able to discern it with your natural eyes**), yet it can cause great problems and pain. It is one of the enemy disguises that are used against you to derail you; it should be discussed in-depth at another time. For now, I will remain focused on the principles for achieving your destiny. I'm pretty sure deception will be discussed in my 2nd book. In several of the following chapters, you will find other disguises of the enemy.

The Principle of Perseverance

We will experience difficult seasons in our lives but you can persevere to your next season and use your experiences to help someone else get their victory. I have shared my miraculous healing in Chapter 4, when the enemy attacked my body (yet God brought me through).
The devil had obviously turned up the heat on me from all directions so; you and I will have to turn it up too.

Remember --- when the accuser backs you in a corner, you got to pick up that Bible (your boxing gloves) and pray the Word on that devil day and night. You might get knocked down but you won't get knocked out because God is your refuge and fortress!!

Life's Goals

Have you experienced any unavoidable obstacles that are preventing you from completing your goal/s or, a project that's still on the shelf? List those goals here that you would like to complete or get started on.

_____

_____

_____

_____

_____

The Principle of Perseverance

Points to review the Perseverance Principle

- *Major setbacks in life can sometimes delay reaching your destiny but keep pressing toward what God has destined for you.*

- *God's plans for you reaching your destiny are always bigger than what we can see.*

- *God will go before you to make every crooked place straight.*

- *Only God can work all of our experiences together whether good or bad to bring about a great outcome.*

- *If you don't succeed the first time, you will have more opportunities to try again.*

- *God will keep you on the potter's wheel until He brings about what He desires out of your life.*

- *There are many battles you don't have to fight when you are willing and obedient to do it God's way.*

- *The enemy will try to use those people closest to you to derail you from achieving your goals.*

CHOSEN

My Dad, the late Joseph Nelson transitioned on to his eternal home, on St. Patrick's Day: March 17, 2009.

Chapter 3

The Principle of PRAYER

Instrumental Bible Characters

Connecting Tracks

Train up a Child

Prayer of Salvation

Review

Prayer

The effective, fervent prayers of a righteous man avails much (b), (James 5:16), nkjv.

"A solemn request for help or expression of thanks addressed to God or an object of worship," (Dictionary.com / Netfind.com).

During the time I lived in Columbia, SC, after I had rededicated my life back to Christ, I had met a young lady at the place of my employment who was part of a prayer group at the church I later joined. Susan had invited me to attend one of their prayer meetings that Friday night at one of the group members' home. They met on alternate Friday evenings and everyone would bring a light snack or dish.

At the prayer meeting one of the seasoned members would expound on the scriptures for about an hour, then prayer request and petitions were given.

The Principle of Prayer

By this time I had been praying on my own, reading the scriptures, and petitioning God about many things in my life. I would not eat on Wednesday's just to have time with God and for prayer. The pastor didn't tell the members to fast on Wednesday but I saw when I did not eat, it drew me closer to God and I saw instant results from my prayers. I was doing it before I really understood the power of fasting and praying in the scriptures.

After the second or third time I attended the prayer meeting, the members inducted me into the prayer group. Those people had a genuine love and passion for what they were doing when they came together. This helped build my prayer life. All of them were powerful prayer warriors and seasoned saints. I had invited one of my close friends to the prayer meeting; we were the babies of the prayer group. Betty and I would keep each other accountable. We prayed together and rode together to the prayer meetings.

CHOSEN

There were several all-night prayer meetings that the pastor allowed the prayer ministry to have at the church. When you leave one of those all-night prayer meetings, you really felt like you were able to take wings and fly!

The tangible manifestation of God's presence still lingered with us as we talked and shared what happened until we reached our destinations.

We saw many of our brothers and sisters prayers answered in that group. It was exciting for both of us to see how God would use the leaders, or even someone who was inspired by the spirit to speak a word, lay hands or rebuke the devil, to deliver someone who needed a touch. We had witnessed various gifts of the spirit operating in the group.

Those people taught me how to stand in the midst of trials and tribulation by using the Word of God. The members taught and lived a life of victory over the enemy. Those were the beginning years when my prayer life started.

Instrumental Bible Characters

In the next section, these Bible Characters were used by God to bring about change and victory through prayer:

David at Ziklag, I Samuel 30: 8, 18-19:
And David inquired of the Lord, saying, Shall I pursue this troop? Shall I overtake them? The Lord answered him, Pursue, for you shall surely overtake them and without fail recover all. David recovered all that the Amalekites had taken and secured his two wives. Nothing was missing, small or great, sons or daughters, spoil or anything that had been taken; David recovered all.

CHOSEN

Elijah defeated the Prophets of Baal, I Kings 18:36-39:

At the time of the offering of the evening sacrifice, Elijah the prophet came near and said, O Lord, the God of Abraham, Isaac, and Israel, let it be known this day that you are God in Israel and that I am Your servant and that I have done all these things at your word. Hear me, O Lord, hear me, that this people may know that you, the Lord are God, and have turned their hearts back to you. Then the fire of the Lord fell and consumed the burnt sacrifice and the wood and the stones and the dust, and also licked up the water that was in the trench. When all the people saw it, they fell on their faces and they said, The Lord He is God! The Lord, He is God!

Hezekiah prayed to God for healing, II Kings 20:1-5:

In those days Hezekiah became deadly ill. The prophet Isaiah son of Amoz came and said to him, Thus says the Lord; Set your house in order, for you shall die; you shall not recover. Then Hezekiah turned his face to the wall and prayed to the Lord, saying, I beseech You, O Lord, earnestly remember now how I have walked before You in faithfulness and truth and with a whole heart entirely devoted to You, and have done what is good in Your sight. And Hezekiah wept bitterly. Before Isaiah had gone out of the Middle court, the word of the Lord came to him; Turn back and tell Hezekiah, the leader of my people, Thus says the Lord, the God of David your (forefather): I have heard your prayer, I have seen your tears; behold, I will heal you. On the third day you shall go up to the house of the Lord.

Hannah prays for a son, I Samuel 1:10 -17 & 20:

And Hannah was in distress of soul, praying to the Lord and weeping bitterly. She vowed, saying, O Lord of hosts, if You will indeed look on the affliction of Your handmaid and earnestly remember, and not forget your handmaid but will give me a son, I will give him to the Lord all his life no razor shall touch his head.

And as she continued praying before the Lord, Eli noticed her mouth. Hannah was speaking in her heart; only her lips moved but her voice was not heard. So Eli thought she was drunk. Eli said to her, how long will you be intoxicated? Put wine away from you.

But Hannah answered, No, my Lord, I am a woman of a sorrowful spirit. I have drunk neither wine nor strong drink, but I was pouring out my soul before the Lord. Regard not your handmaid as a wicked woman; for out of my great complaint and bitter provocation I have been speaking. Then Eli said, Go in peace, and may the God of Israel grant your petition which you have asked of Him. Hannah became pregnant and in due time bore a son and named him Samuel (heard of God), because, she said, I have asked him of the Lord.

Paul & Silas prayed & sang praises to God, Acts 16:25-26:

But about midnight, as Paul and Silas were praying and singing hymns of praise to God, and the other prisoners were listening to them. Suddenly there was a great earthquake, so that the very foundations of the prison were shaken; and at once all the doors were opened and everyone's shackles were unfastened.

Connecting Tracks

During the Christmas Holidays, I love going to the malls to sight see all of the beautiful Christmas decorations. Once you walk through the doors, you are captivated by the blinking bright colorful lights, the smell of pine cones and cinnamon is in the air. The feeling and comfort at Christmas time is here! It looks so wonderful with mistletoes, berries, red ribbons & bows, gold and green ribbons and ornaments everywhere. Santa was seated high in the corner riding a big red shining sleigh with his reindeers.

There were big beautiful Christmas trees decorated in various colors and sizes placed in several areas of the mall. You can spend all day there just enjoying the various views of Christmas decorations.

Some of the Christmas trees were changing colors and there was a Christmas jingle with every changing color ….. just beautiful!

Then I was amazed to see at the bottom of one of the biggest trees in the Mall a slow moving train circling the beautiful tree.

The train continued circling the area and gave a toot and a puff of white smoke as it rolled along the track. I thought as my eyes were fixed on that train ---- I noticed that it didn't have the connecting tracks that would allow the train to change tracks. The circling train below the Christmas tree at the Mall reminded me of the days I waited at the train station when I lived in Boston.

There was the main track alongside the station but several miles in the distance you could see several other tracks connecting from various cities traveling to other nearby cities transporting riders.

The riders would say that when the train arrived at the station late it was because the trains had to change tracks to allow the other trains to get to other areas of the city.

Just as those trains I rode in Boston, to and from various destinations, to the single train I saw circling the big Christmas tree at the mall; they both reminded me of our destiny.

We have to get on several trains going in several different areas and destinations to reach our destiny. When you are *chosen* you may start off on that single track circling one area but when you begin to grow and mature in the things of God, you cannot remain on that same track, you will have to change tracks to get all that God has for you.

Tweet this ... "Another trick of the enemy, he will try to isolate you to that one track, for years, wherein you are repeatedly circling the same area but going nowhere."

You may look fine and very handsome and even smell good, you may even think that you're some-kind-of-wonderful, but the truth is, if you're not on the connecting track, then stop this cycle now. You have lost focus. **Recalculating.**

God's plan for your life is so great, He has to get us connected to various tracks so you can continue to grow and bring forth fruit that will remain.

> *By this My Father is glorified, that you bear much fruit; so you will be my disciples. You did not choose Me, but I chose you and appointed you that you should go and bear fruit, and that your fruit should remain, that whatever you ask the Father in My name He may give you*
> *(Jn. 15:8 & 16) nkjv.*

Train up a child in the way he should go

The Evangelism Ministry returned back to the church around 12:30pm that Saturday because it had started raining while we were out in the community.

The leaders advised us to finish early due to the weather. I had taken a call from one of my sisters when I returned to the church and what I was told was not very clear. I couldn't figure out what had happened, being in Atlanta and not having all the information.

My sister who had called didn't have all the details either. She only knew that one of our sister's children was taken into foster care.

I was working in foster care for about 5 years during that time and I had witnessed and seen various forms of anxiety and depression, as children were removed from their parents and families.

I used the Diagnostic and Statistical Manual (DSM) during my tenure in graduate school and had only picked up that book about two times since graduation. I didn't have enough information about my sister's situation to make an accurate assessment that would bring her any relief.

Weakness filled my stomach and my knees began to shake after I took the call.

The evangelism team had a good day of ministering to those who wanted prayer and some who had received salvation. I requested prayer from the team for my sister in distress and for myself because I knew somehow she would get through this with prayer.

After my family had gathered all the details about what had happened, we decided that we would go and support my sister and spend a few days with her and the family.
We traveled all evening that Sunday and arrived at my sister's home around 1:00am.

My sister appeared to have slipped into a state of depression and decided that she didn't want to talk or eat. We had to really encourage her and her husband, and then we decided to do what Paul & Silas did in Acts 16 (we didn't know what else to do and most of the allegations in the report was a fabrication).

I advised my sister and brother-in-law all that I learned since I also worked for the state of GA in family and children services. Although the state where they lived was involved, no state is a match to what God can do in his sovereignty and power.
My family worshipped and prayed every morning and even though the staff members and supervisors had another plan for when

the children could be returned home, "they said." But, **on the 3rd day**, the children (my nieces) were returned home after school.

M-I-S-S-I-O-N A-C-C-O-M-P-L-I-S-H-E-D!

Yes, **God did it!** I told my mom about the dream I had early that Wednesday morning, but I could not make any sense of it. I saw in my dream about four people, of different nationalities, in a parked car near the side of the road.

It appeared that they had all shot and killed each other; there were no one left living in the car. I could tell from the scene in my dream, it was not a car accident anywhere in sight. The vehicle looked fine, but all the people inside the car were wounded and lifeless.

In this last section of the prayer chapter, you will have an opportunity to recite the sinner's prayer so you too can continue to produce fruit that will remain in your life.

And you will be able to accomplish those things that God has purposed just for you. If you have not recited the sinner's prayer before to receive Jesus in your heart, this will be the best thing that you could ever do in your life.

You have read in this chapter about the power of prayer from several Bible Characters and you have seen the results of prayer when my nieces were returned home to their parents.

We all need someone bigger than we are to work things out on our behalf; you cannot reach your destiny and goals alone.

Prayer of Salvation

Now is your time, and remember, the single track that's not going anywhere is a good example of where the unproductive cycles in your life should end. You are destined for greatness, you are *chosen*, and you want to be a recipient of all that God has for you, so

The Principle of Prayer

you would need to get on the connecting track.

If you are already a believer, then you can move on to the Faith Principle in Chapter 4

We all have 5 senses, we all have emotions, and we all have experienced pain and disappointments on various levels. Some have done good deeds, some have sung soulful stirring songs, and your service to the needy can not replace salvation. You can not save yourself. So let's take care of this now.

You can be comforted in this decision; it's just like A, B, C.

CHOSEN

<u>A</u> - Accept that the sacrifice Jesus completed on the cross was for you (death, burial, resurrection).

<u>B</u> - Believe that Jesus is God's son who was sent to save the world from their sins and reunite you back to Him, repent of your sins (only someone who couldn't have sinned could do this).

<u>C</u> - Confess with your mouth and believe in your heart that you are now saved.

For God so greatly loved and dearly prized the world that He gave up His only begotten son, so that whoever believes in (trusts in, clings to, relies on) Him shall not perish, come to destruction or lost but have eternal everlasting life (John 3:16), amp.

———————————

The Principle of Prayer

Because if you acknowledge and confess with your mouth that Jesus is Lord and believe in your heart (adhere to, trust in, and rely on the truth) that God raised Jesus from the dead, you will be saved. For with the heart a person believes and so is justified and with the mouth the confession of salvation (Rom. 10:9&10), amp.

If you have confessed the Sinners Prayer for the first time, then the angels in heaven are rejoicing with you! I am too! Please sign your name and date here. This will be your new spiritual birthday.

_____

Born Again, this _____ day of _____, year_____.

There are several devotional readings and spiritual journals that can help you with your prayer life at your local book store, Christian book stores and Walmart too. You can also find daily devotional readings online. Don't forget to read your bible daily. The scriptures will also help you to become a strong prayer warrior.

CHOSEN

Also praying with a friend or prayer partner will start the growth process. And the most important thing --- please find a church that you can attend weekly so you can grow (I Peter 2:2) and be among other believers.

WELCOME TO THE FAMILY OF FAITH !

Share your new birth experience with a friend or family member.

(Read Luke 15:10 & Colossians 2:10)

The Principle of Prayer

"Father God, thank you so much for my sister/brother who you have *chosen* to be in the family of faith. I thank you Father that the enemy no longer has control over my sister/ brother's life because they are now washed with the Precious Blood of Jesus. Father God, continue to show yourself strong and mighty in their lives, knowing that everything they touch will prosper. Father, keep them in your care for you have engraved them in the palm of your hand, as you manifest your holy spirit in them. And let her/him know that no weapon formed against you shall prosper.

Father, thank you now that their lives are a blessing to you and too many others, and their future is secure, in Jesus Name. Amen."

Make prayer a daily priority ....

Points to review for the Prayer Principle

- ✓ Prayer is needed and vital for daily living.

- ✓ Prayer is always effective in a group or by yourself.

- ✓ God can demonstrate His supernatural powers when the saints come together in prayer agreement.

- ✓ The gifts of the spirit are seen during prayer meetings.

- ✓ Your life will be victorious through prayer.

- ✓ David recovered all his possessions and wives from the Amalekites at Ziklag after he prayed.

- ✓ The Fire of God fell and defeated Baal's prophets after Elijah prayed.

- ✓ Hannah prayed for a son and God heard her prayer and blessed her with a son, Samuel.

- ✓ Paul and Silas was supernaturally released from jail after praying and singing praises to God.

The Principle of Prayer

- ✓ *Everyone should desire to get on the connecting track that you can have access to all that God has for you.*

- ✓ *God can do the impossible even when all odds are against you.*

- ✓ *There is purposeful power in prayer to receive salvation.*

CHOSEN

My friend and prayer partner, Betty Simmons transitioned on to her eternal rest on: May 23, 2015.

Chapter 4

The Principle of FAITH

Predestined

Prayer & Faith

Cheryl's Miraculous Healing

Fear of the unknown

John Smith Story

Your Testimony

Review

CHOSEN

Faith

Now faith is the substance of things hoped for, the evidence of things not seen (Hebrews 11:1), nkjv.

"Complete trust or confidence in someone or something," (Dictionary.com / Merriam-Webster.com).

The Faith principle is *very* important for you to understand. Having Faith will allow you to activate, achieve or obtain *all* that God has predestined for you (all of your goals, dreams and your destiny has to be achieved by faith).
There are many things in life that you will acquire and achieve without having faith ….. but, **your God given goals and destiny will *"only"* be obtained by faith. Without faith, it is impossible to please God (Heb. 11:6).**

Many of us will experience numerous days of difficulties, unexpected defeat and sometimes even failure but you can still reach your destiny.

You can not give up now; you have to be persistent and intentional about getting what God has for you.

Remember this ---- stay focused on the track of discipline and perseverance then you will be able to achieve all of your goals.

> *For we are God's own handiwork, His workmanship, recreated in Christ Jesus, (born anew) that we may do those good works which God predestined (planned beforehand) for us (taking paths which He prepared ahead of time), that we should walk in them, living the good life which He prearranged and made ready for us to live (Eph. 2:10), amp*

Predestined means: before, prior to, in advance of, beforehand. Purposed, predetermined and spoken into existence concerning you (Dictionary.com).

God's plans for your life are great; it's secured, and it was tailored just for you. A seamstress will take all of your measurements if you were getting a garment made.

CHOSEN

In the event the garment is not coming together as planned, you may need to return to the seamstress to have the measurements altered or redone.

There may be several fittings and alterations until the desired garment fits properly. The final outcome here is, you want to be comfortable in the garment and also, you want to look fine wearing it …. right?

That's very similar to what God does with **His** plans for our future and destiny. Unlike the seamstress, God doesn't make any alterations to His plan. God's plans for you and me were completed before we were conceived. You can trust that God knows all about you better than you know yourself!

God's plans are to bless you. Everything about you has already been factored in, (Egypt, Baal, Plagues, Ishmael, Prison, Goliath, Delilah, Tarshish, Bethesda).

The Principle of Faith

Yes, and all the other bad, nasty or distasteful stuff you're not proud of, were also factored in to God's plans.

God already know the way you would take. Your plan "B" ---- is God's plan "A!" (Rom. 8:28; Prov. 19:21).

No one can take or change what God has purposed for you, because it's for you. It will fit you well. You were already *chosen* for it. That's always comforting for me to know, that God's plans for me are good, (and not of evil).

For I know the plans I have for you,
declares the LORD, plans to prosper you and
not to harm you, plans to give you hope
and a future (Jer. 29:11), niv.

CHOSEN

Your parents, your friends, your sister, your brother, your neighbors, your coworkers, your man, your woman, or even your manager can't change it (I wanted to list everyone who will try). **But, let me drop this on you, right here** …. those people in your life and even the devil will try to change what God has predestined for you.

The enemy will try to rob you of God's blessings for your life and even your destiny. The devil wants you to follow him or her; the enemy doesn't want you to follow God's plan and be blessed or even be a blessing to others.

Also, the devil's plan can be very appealing to your flesh and your five senses (never think that you are able to beat the devil in your own strength) you will lose that fight ….. **every time**.

The devil already knows how he or she can defeat you. Here's another scripture to help you ..... **Submit yourselves, then, to God. Resist the devil, and he will flee from you** (James 4:7).

If you are hanging out with the devil, guess what.... (Mom would use these words to get her point across). "Nine- times- out- of- ten," the devil already got the best of you. The devil can trick you and slick you so quick, you may think it's from God, but the devil is a liar!

Here's another revelation, **the devil will even take you to church!** If you are not careful and discerning the right spirit you could easily follow satan, down a road of destruction and miss what God has purposed for you.

The thief comes only in order to steal and kill and destroy. I came that they may have and enjoy life, and have it in abundance, to the full, till it overflows (John 10:10), amp.

The scripture in II Timothy 2:15, is important for you to remember. You have to study God's Word and meditate on the Word to get what's yours. You can't tell the devil what your momma or grand-momma said about the Word. You have to have the Word in your own heart to fight the good fight of faith. If you are knowledgeable of what the Word says about you, then you have all that's needed to defeat the devil.

On the other hand, if you are not knowledgeable of the Word you will be defeated in many areas of your life.

As we have learned through the scriptures, the Word brought healing, miracles, multiplication, protection, conviction and even peace was spoken by the Word.

For the weapons of our warfare are not carnal, flesh, but mighty through God to the pulling down of strong holds (II Corth. 10:4), kjv.

Once you know the Word, you can pray the Word and practice the Word daily.

The Principle of Faith

***Your prayers and your life of faith
can change any situation.***

Your prayers can change things for the people in your circle, a family member or a love one who is being beat-up by the enemy. Some of them may be an immature believer and some of them may not have accepted Jesus in their life yet.

But you are strong enough in the faith now so, you will start praying for salvation and rebuke the devil on their behalf, because you already know what the Word has done for you. And the Word will do the same for someone who you are praying for also.

The word and your faith brings benefits.

When Jesus had entered Capernaum, a centurion came to him, asking for help. "Lord," he said, "my servant lies at home paralyzed, suffering terribly." Jesus said to him, "Shall I come and heal him?" The Centurion replied, "Lord, I do not deserve to have you come under my roof.

But just say the word, and my servant will be healed. For I myself am a man under authority, with soldiers under me. I tell this one, "go," and he goes; and that one, "come," and he comes. I say to my servant, "do this," and he does it." When Jesus heard this, He was amazed and said to those following him, "Truly I tell you, I have not found anyone in Israel with such great faith. Then Jesus said to the centurion, "Go! Let it be done just as you believed it would." And his servant was healed at that moment (Matt. 8:5-10 & 13), niv.

Prayer & Faith

Faith will always follow prayer because once you have prayed about anything, than you will need to use your faith to see God bring the manifested answer. Faith can also be used before you pray to get the same results.

So, you will find that prayer and faith goes hand-in-hand on your chosen righteous path that God has predestined just for you.

The Principle of Faith

I will show you in the next section of the faith principle what happens when you put your faith to work. As you begin to grow in your faith and embrace righteousness, my hopes for you are that you will strive for STRONG faith. This will ALWAYS bring manifested answers …..

> *And Jesus said to him, "Go your way; " your faith has made you well." And immediately he recovered his sight and followed him on the way (Mark 10:52), esv.*

Cheryl's Miraculous Healing

I had attended the one night healing service at our church on September 28, 2016. Pastor David Turner was the guest Pastor and he called several people to the pulpit for prayer. He laid hands and prayed for the sick and rebuked the devil, and many were healed, set free and delivered that Wednesday night at New Birth.

I sat there taking notes and recording the scriptures as I usually do, but that night in particular, I had a strange feeling and fear rushed over my soul. I knew there was a problem in my body but I didn't know what it was.

As I recalled that moment and time sitting there, I later found out that I had a serious problem in my right breast that I didn't know about then. What was odd about the whole thing was, it was first revealed to me sitting there in that healing service.

For several days following, I started to feel discomfort and pain in my right breast. I was about to lose my mind because it took about 2 weeks to get an appointment with my doctor. I had received a good report from my mammogram screening in April of 2016, so, I had to bring my faith in alignment with what I had already known about the Word and being a servant of The Most High God; He is a healer.

***I had to keep my faith attached to
my previous prayer history and
referenced all that God had already
done in my life through prayer and faith.***

This may become difficult when the devil starts working on your emotions and anxiety, then fear creeps in. But, this wasn't any different or any bigger than anything else that God had showed up in.
I know God is a healer! I had prayed and cried with many with this type of problem and there were even coworkers and family members who were getting treatment during this time and I became very fearful of what was next for me.

I had asked two of the women elders at church one Sunday to pray with me and from that day until this day, my body was miraculously healed.

I knew I had a problem, I knew the symptoms were there, I knew my doctor ordered more sonogram testing but I can say that --- **Jesus did it!** It was like I went through major surgery but without getting a cut and no anesthesia!!

I told my family and the ladies that prayed with me that I felt like God had given me new boobs!! Yes, He did. God completed my healing on October 26, 2016.

I sat in my car that Wednesday evening before Bible study sharing my testimony with a friend. I felt a renewal in my body that something was different from before. It was such an AWESOME thing that only God could do, **H-a-l-l-e-l-u-j-a-h-**!!

As I was nearing the time for my mammogram for the year 2017, of course I was getting fearful and nervous again. And you know the devil was trying to fool me that I wasn't healed.

I had all kinds of crazy thoughts going through my head and I had to tell the devil, "God has already healed me and you can't take it from me !!"

You got to talk to that devil and let him know that God is greater than he is. And if he comes back, you got to tell him again, louder and stronger than before.

Fear of the unknown

Here is another hidden disguise of the enemy... **FEAR** (False Evidence Appearing Real). That devil will create so much fear and anxiety in you in order to change the course of God's plans for you. Fear can be crippling if you are not in control of your emotions.

Jesus continually spoke to His disciples about fear, and He reminds us also in His Word that fear has torment, replace your fear with love. Agape love will cover any form of fear.

When fear tries to control anything concerning you, remember God's love is greater and you have to rest in His care and His plans for "**you**." You can not afford to compare yourself with anyone else.

Whatever your mother, father, brother, sister, uncle, aunt, grandparents, friends or coworkers had to endure was by God's grace and mercy.

God has given you authority to break any curse that's operating in your family (we have to use the Word). Whatever He brought you and me through is by God's grace and mercy.

Fear can also prevent you from reaching your destiny. You maybe desiring to take on a new venture or assignment to achieve one of your goals, but fear of the unknown blocks your movement. And you began to recite all that fear has done to you.

The Principle of Faith

I won't be able to finish my degree or even pass a test at my age; I can't afford that car on my salary; I'm not smart enough to take the SAT; I was raised by a single parent; My feet are too big to be a model; None of my siblings stayed with their spouses; My dad died when I was a child; I'm too shy to pray in public; All of my uncles used drugs, now I'm addicted; I'm too tired to exercise; They won't give me a loan, I have bad credit, etc.

Before you know it (speak words of life), you have agreed with fear and it's become a strong-hold in you (Isa. 41:10, II Tim. 1:7, Psa. 27:1-3).

Fear can easily block your view from moving forward but you have to step up to the plate and ….. **S-W-I-N-G**. The first step may be difficult if fear has crippled you, but keep swinging until you make contact. Once you get started, stay the course, you will win in the end.

Does any of those fear tactics sounds like what you are saying or what you said?

Take the first step of faith and stay the course, you will win in the end.

For all the promises of God in Him are Yes, and in Him Amen, to the glory of God through us (II Corth. 1:20), nkjv

The "John Smith" Story

This video was viewed at New Birth Church a few years ago as Bishop Long gave a faith-filled sermon that day.

On Jan. 19, 2015 around 11:35 am, three boys were seen walking on the icy Lake Sainte Louise in O'Fallon, Missouri, when the boys fell through the ice. One of the boys was able to swim back to shore and got out of the water, the second boy was rescued by the police.

The Principle of Faith

The third boy "**John Smith**" was reported as being under water for 15 minutes; he was rescued and taken to the hospital.

The 14 years old, John Smith had no pulse and was not breathing for about 20 minutes. The rescue team completed 15 minutes of CPR but to no avail. The doctors continue to work on him for about 27 minutes to revive him, but the child did not show any signs of life.

The report stated that the doctors brought the child's mother in to inform her of her son's death; then the mother, Joyce Smith began to pray aloud, "God please don't take my son, come Holy Spirit, I want my son, please send your spirit to save my son."

The mother reported that she could not remember all that she said or prayed, but she didn't want her son to die, "As published in the St. Louis Post-Dispatch, 1-21-15."

The Doctors were amazed to see the child's heart was "jumped started" by the Holy Spirit when his mother prayed.

The mother continued to pray until life was returned to her son.

One doctor said within a matter of a minute or two after the mother had prayed, the child's heart started again, "As published in the St. Louis Post-Dispatch, 1-21-15."

John Smith amazing recovery was nothing the Doctors have ever seen; they said it was a bonafide miracle, "As published in the St. Louis Post-Dispatch, 1-21-15."

> For I will contend with him who contends with you, and I will save your children (Isa. 49:25-b), nkjv.

Apparently, Mrs. Smith's life of prayer and faith saved her son's life. The report stated that she continued to pray until life was returned to her son; she knew the power of prayer. Mrs. Smith put her faith to work and she was not disappointed with the manifested results.

Take your faith to the next level when you are given a bad report.

What do you think would have happened had Mrs. Smith not prayed after the doctor's report?

Your Testimony

I know you have a few testimonies also that only God could have done. It doesn't have to be a healing of infirmity or disease; it could have been restoration of a marriage or dead relationship. It could have been a bad deal went wrong and God turned it in your favor. It could have been a difficult test that you thought you would fail but you passed it. It could have been the foreclosure of your home was canceled. It could have been when you were signing divorce papers, and God changed your spouse's heart.

It could have been a difficult supervisor or an employee that God gave you the patience to work with. It could have been one of your children that you thought you wanted to send him or her back to Jesus, and God stepped in just in time. It could have been finances or grants needed for college, or a business, and somehow it was taken care of.

CHOSEN

And they overcame him by the blood of the Lamb and by the word of their testimony (Rev. 12:11), nkjv.

God has all kinds of miraculous ways to bless you. Leave your difficult situations in the hands of God, I guarantee you, He will turn it in your favor!

On the lines below, think about two of your blessings that you know only God could have done ... or, a situation when God turned it in your favor, when you knew the odds were against you. You can record dates and time also if you remember them.

The Principle of Faith

You will be able to reference "**your testimony**" as needed, if someone asks you to share one.

_____

_____

_____

_____

_____

_____

_____

Saying, if you will diligently hearken to the voice of the Lord your God and will do what is right in His sight, and will listen to and obey His commandments and keep all His statures, I will put none of the diseases upon you which I brought upon the Egyptians, for I am the Lord who heals you (Exod. 15:26), amp.

Points to review for the Faith Principle

- ✓ You will achieve your destiny by faith.

- ✓ Having faith will help you rise above life's difficulties and obstacles.

- ✓ Your destiny was predestined and spoken over your life by faith.

- ✓ The devil will try to rob you of your faith and your destiny to follow him so you won't get what God has for you.

- ✓ Grow your faith by studying the Word so you won't be fooled by the enemy.

- ✓ You will use spiritual weapons, not carnal weapons to stay focused on your destiny.

- ✓ Your faith can change your loved one's situation when you intercede in prayer for them.

- ✓ Faith and prayer go hand-in-hand to accomplish what God has predestined for you.

- ✓ Fear can prevent you from moving forward in faith, wherein you won't achieve your goals.

Chapter 5

The Principle of HUMILITY

Jesus's Birth

Characters of Jesus

Family Dynamics

Humility Situation

Review

CHOSEN

Humility

Therefore humble yourself under the mighty hand of God, that he may exalt you in due time (1 Peter 5:6), nkjv.

"Freedom from pride or arrogance, the quality or state of being humble," (Merriam-Webster.com / Dictionary.com).

Have you ever thought about "where" and "how" your parents brought you into the world when you were born? Some people can share the account of how long their mother was in labor, the people who accompanied her and /or your parents during your delivery.

Others would say, "I'm a Grady Baby" or they will use the hospital name where they were born. What about those people who say that they were born in the front seat or the back seat of their parent's car, or in the ambulance.

The Principle of Humility

And some may say that they were born at home with a midwife, while others were born in the taxi cab, because you just couldn't wait to make your grand entrance to see what you've waited for so long, after 9 months!

Many people are able to give a full story about their birth and they know the day of the week, the weather conditions, the time, even down to the very seconds surrounding their birth. Your birth was such a memorable time that it's one that your mother and /or your parents won't ever forget.

After you have read this section on *humility*, it would be a good opportunity for you to talk with your mother or your parents to understand the situation surrounding your birth. Your birth may have been, very painful, horrific, exciting, traumatic, or some would say, a mistake, yet your birth was a humbling experience for your mother and/or parents.

Whatever the situation was surrounding your birth should be very humbling for all of us, just to know that we survived! And you were not a mistake; let's straighten that out right here.

You have a purpose and destiny to fulfill, even if you feel like you don't belong. If your parents are no longer living, then maybe someone in your family knows about your birth. We were taught to speak life over our birthday, **"It does matter that you were born!"**

> *You saw me before I was born. Every day of my life was recorded in your book. Every moment was laid out before a single day had passed (Psa. 139:16), nlt.*

Jesus Humble Birth

That introduction was *chosen* to get you to think about the situation surrounding Jesus's Birth ….. "hum." God had *chosen* Jesus's Mother (Mary) and his natural Father (Joseph) to be the parents of Jesus.

And he chose the date, time and place where our Savior, the Messiah would be born.

It was already prophesied about Jesus's birth, the crucifixion and His resurrection, and at the appointed time it was all fulfilled (Isa. 7:14, Matt. 1:22-23, Gal. 4:4-5, Isa. 53:7, Matt. 28:5-6).

We always envision the Nativity scene when someone speaks about Jesus's birth. We have heard many sermons about Jesus's birth usually during the Christmas holidays. It's always exciting during the Christmas season to spend time with our families and love ones and to enjoy Christmas carols, exchanging gifts and the beautiful lights at Christmas time. But when we think of that Nativity scene, it brings us back to, **"humility."**

The descriptions and place of Jesus's birth was said by many pastors as: Jesus was born in a horse stable or a barn, and Mary & Joseph laid Him in a trough or manger where the horses and cattle would eat; some say that Jesus was born out back of the Inn (guest house), because there were no vacancy; others say that Jesus was born where the shepherds watch over the sheep, goats and pigs grazing in the field.

All of those sermons could have possibly described the place where Jesus was born, and we all must agree that it was not one of normalcy. So, the main point here is Jesus's humble entry into the world, this was God's plan.

What should we learn about Jesus's birth that could help us in our own humanity ....

And Joseph also went up from Galilee from the town of Nazareth to Judea, to the town of David, which is called Bethlehem, because he was of the house and family of David. To be enrolled with Mary, his espoused, married wife, who was about to become a mother. And while they were there, the time came for her delivery, and she gave birth to her Son, her Firstborn; and she wrapped Him in swaddling clothes and laid Him in a manger, because there was no room or

The Principle of Humility

place for them in the inn. And in that vicinity there were shepherds living out under the open sky in the field, watching in shifts over their flock by night. And behold, an angel of the Lord stood by them and the glory of the Lord flashed and shone all about them, and they were terribly frightened (Luke 2:4-9), amp.

If you had to complete a survey of, "why did Jesus, our Savior had to enter the world the way that He did?" I believe many of the responses to the survey would reference the word, **"Humble or Humility."** I am sure you will get various astounding responses, but I'm convinced now that our Savior's entry into the world was to teach us all about **humility**.

> *He was despised and rejected and forsaken by men, a Man of sorrows and pains and acquainted with grief and sickness; and like One from Whom men hide their faces He was despised, and we did not appreciate His worth or have any esteem for Him (Isa. 53:3),* amp.

CHOSEN

The Character of Jesus

Let's look at some names for JESUS, as He came to earth in a very humble abode; His name is described in many ways to show his Power, Authority & Divinity.

Jesus is called, the Anointed One, All Knowing and All Powerful, the Mighty God, The Lion of Judah, the First and the Last, Alpha & Omega and many others. We serve a powerful and mighty God and Jesus being our example took on human form and divinity, yet He humbled himself even to the death of the cross. We must also take on the character as Jesus did to show others, saved or unsaved that our lives are also submitted under God.

The believer's life is one that is humbly submitted under the powerful hands of the All Mighty God.

The Principle of Humility

I have been crucified with Christ and I no longer live, but Christ lives in me. The life I now live in the body, I live by faith in the Son of God, who loved me and gave himself for me (Gal. 2:20), niv.

Throughout the scriptures Jesus shows us various definition of his character when he uses, forgiveness, love, servitude and humility. Jesus spoke with the disciples about being great in the kingdom:

He called a little child to him, and placed the child among them. And He said: Truly I tell you, unless you change and become like little children, you will never enter the kingdom of heaven. Therefore, whoever takes the lowly position of this child is the greatest in the kingdom of heaven (Matt. 18:2-4), niv.

Jesus used humility when He healed the blind man:

And he charged them that they should tell no man; but the more he charged them, so much the more a great deal they published it (Mark 7:36), erv.

God speaks of forgiveness and humility when you pray.

If my people, which are called by my name, shall humble themselves, and pray, and seek my face, and turn from their wicked ways; then will I hear from heaven, and will forgive their sin, and will heal their land (2 Chron. 7:14), kjv.

We see how the Bible characters used humility in order for God to restore them and put them back on the path that was *chosen* for him or her. So, we should remain humble too to get all that God has for us. **Pride, disobedience and unforgiveness** remains at the top of the list that hinders us from being humbled.

The **Identity principle** in chapter 7 will also be very important for you to understand concerning obtaining your destiny. Your true identity encompasses all that God made you to be and who "**He**" said that you are **(fearfully and wonderfully made)**.

Humility was woven into your identity and remains a part of who you are and also for you to become more like Jesus.

The Principle of Humility

A man's pride will bring him low: but honor shall uphold the humble in spirit (Pro. 29:23), kjv.

In the next section, let's discuss the Does' family dynamics and how Mrs. Gillcuttie used humility.

Doe's Family Dynamics

Mr. John & Mrs. Jane Doe were married for 10 years now. They have three beautiful children: Jessica 8 years old, John Jr 5 years old, & Janice 2 years old. The family has been attending The Rising Dove Baptist Church for several years but lately Mrs. Jane Doe cannot get her husband to go to church with the family. She asked the pastor and church family to pray for Mr. Doe and her family as she wiped the tears from her eyes. Mr. John Doe had missed several days from work and he never arrives on time.

CHOSEN

The Supervisor, Mrs. Gillcuttie reported when Mr. Doe is in the office he is not meeting deadlines for major projects. She said that several of Mr. Doe's reports were returned to him for correction and verification.

Mr. Doe has been seen hanging out with his buddies after work at the bar and not coming home until late. Mrs. Jane Doe has voiced her concerns to her husband several times but to no avail has she seen any changes in husband's behavior.

Mr. John Doe was summoned to the office last Friday by his director due to his work was not meeting company's standards and he was not meeting deadlines. Mr. Doe was given a written warning.

Mrs. Jane Doe decided that she and their three children would go live with her parents in Macon until Mr. John Doe can get his self together and be the father and husband that he needs to be to his family.

The Principle of Humility

Over several weeks now Mr. John Doe started parking his car two streets over from his home in a neighbor's garage at night. Mr. Doe have had several calls from the bank loan officer due to his car payment is now three months behind for his 2015 sports BMW, X5 series.

Mr. John Doe had contacted his mother-in-law to ask her to talk with her daughter (his wife), and convince Jane to reconsider allowing him to have visits with the children. Mrs. Doe reiterates that she decided not to have the children father to visit with them any longer due to he talks bad about her, and calls her derogatory names to the children and he blames her for their separation.

Mr. Doe's director and manager had given him 30 days to get his act together but nothing had changed since his written reprimand.

CHOSEN

The director sent Mrs. R. Gillcuttie an email to terminate Mr. Doe's employment when he comes into the office this morning.

Scenario A:

Supervisor, Mrs. Gillcuttie sent Mr. John Doe an email at 9:45am when she noticed that he had arrived at the office. Mr. Doe's start time for work is 9:00am.

Good morning Mr. John Doe,

This note is to inform you to come by my office after the receipt of this email.
Thank You,

Mrs. R. Gillcuttie,
Unit Supervisor

Mr. Doe goes by the break room for a cup of coffee and said good morning to his coworkers; he arrives at Mrs. Gillcuttie's office around 10:05am.

The Principle of Humility

Good morning Mrs. Gillcuttie, you wanted to see me?

Mr. Doe ... come to the conference room for a few minutes ..... (he noticed the stern look on her face).

Mrs. Gillcuttie, is there a staff meeting this morning, or is something wrong?

Yes, you're fired!! ... effective immediately!! We've tried to help you Mr. Doe, but since you choose not to accept the company's help when you were given the written reprimand ... and, my goodness, you're always late! Here's your exit papers...... clean out your desk now! And leave the premise! Don't forget to turn in your keycard at the security desk!

CHOSEN

Scenario B:

Supervisor Mrs. Gillcuttie sent Mr. John Doe an email around 9:45am when she noticed that he had arrived at the office. Mr. Doe's start time at work is 9:00am.

Good morning Mr. Doe,

This note is to inform you to come by my office after the receipt of this email.

See you then,

Mrs. R. Gillcuttie
Unit Supervisor

Mr. Doe arrives at Mrs. Gillcuttie's office around 10:05, after he got a cup of coffee and said good morning to his coworkers.

The Principle of Humility

Good morning Mrs. Gillcuttie, you wanted to see me?

Good Morning Mr. Doe, yes ... please, come to the conference room for a few minutes.

Mrs. Gillcuttie, is there a staff meeting this morning, or is something wrong?

No ---- there's not a staff meeting this morning but ... I was given directives from the director so...., the agency will have to terminate your employment this morning.

And, I have your separation papers right here. I'm so sorry about this Mr. Doe .... But, is everything OK with you and your family? It appears that you've been having some personal problems.....

Well, "I'm having some problems ... yea, I am." But please don't tell anyone .... "me and my wife are separated right now".... (Mr. Doe held his head down and became emotional).

CHOSEN

"But -- I'm - gonna-- get -- it - together -- Mrs. Gillcuttie." Sorry to hear that Mr. Doe, I will be praying for you and your family.

OK, please make sure you stop by my office before you leave and take your time to clean out your office. I can give your keycard to security.
I will ….. thank you Mrs. Gillcuttie, I would appreciate that.

From the Doe's Family Dynamics, which scenario would be the best form of **humility** to terminate Mr. Doe's employment ?

_____ A   or   _____ B

The Principle of Humility

Let nothing be done through selfish ambition or conceit, but in lowliness of mind let each esteem others better than himself. Let each of you look out not only for his own interests, but also for the interests of others (Phil. 2:3-4), njkv.

In the spaces provided below, think about a situation in your life or your career, when you used **"humility"** towards someone when you were in a position of power...

_____

_____

_____

_____

_____

_____

CHOSEN

Points to review for the Humility Principle

- *The circumstances surrounding the time and the place of your birth were already known by God.*

- *The prophesied place of Jesus's birth in the Nativity scene was God's plan to show the world humility.*

- *Jesus is all-powerful and all-knowing yet he humbled himself to glorify his father, even to the death of the cross.*

- *Jesus taught about being great in the kingdom is to become humbled like a child.*

- *Humility and forgiveness is needed when we petition God in prayer.*

- *Humility should always be used when you are in a positon of power; use your position to build up and not to destroy.*

- *Think of ways you could incorporate humility in your daily activities.*

Chapter 6

The Principle of SERVING

Servanthood Characteristics

Jesus being a Servant

Serving in Ministry

Servanthood Activity

Review

CHOSEN

Serving

For even the Son of Man came not to be served but to serve, and to give his life as a ransom for many (Mark 10:45), esv.

"A person who performs duties for others, especially a person employed in a house on domestic duties or as a personal attendant," **(Merriam-Webster.com / Dictionary.com).**

When I consider having a servant's heart or serving, I'm reminded of the scripture:

Whatever you do, work at it wholeheartedly as though you were doing it for the Lord and not merely for people, knowing that from the Lord you will receive the inheritance as your reward (Col. 3:23-24), isv.

My "side-gig" or job where I work on weekends reminds me of having a servant's heart. The job itself is not too bad but one disconcerting thing about it is being on my feet for hours and carrying those heavy trays.

The Principle of Serving

The main goal here is to ensure the guests have everything they need for a wonderful evening. Whatever the guest calls for, a napkin, water, silverware, a glass of tea, it's my responsibility to go get it, and get it quickly. If I can't get it, then I should go to someone who can get it for the guest, in a minimal amount of time.

The main objective here is to make the guests happy even if I feel reduced to being a slave for these, "boujee people." It doesn't matter if one of my eye-lashes are about to fall off, or even my feet may be screaming for relief, someone else's needs are my main priority.

Servanthood Characteristics

When we consider serving or being a servant, there are several characteristics that comes to mind, and usually it is very obvious when someone doesn't have the right attitude while serving, they stick out like a sore thumb.

Here are a few characteristics of someone being a servant that you will be able to recognize very easily: patience, loyalty, disciplined, loving, faithful, kind, humbled, mature, forgiving, longsuffering, to name a few. Add additional characteristics here:

_____, _____, _____.

Jesus being a Servant

Since Jesus is our ultimate example of being a servant, let's look at some of the ways He served His disciples and the people.

Jesus having a servant's heart as He washes the disciple's feet: **John 13:3-5 & 14-16.**

Jesus knew that the Father had put all things under his power, and that he had come from God and was returning to God: so He got up from the meal, took off his outer clothing, and wrapped a towel around his waist. After that, He poured water into a basin and began to wash His disciples' feet, drying them with the towel that was wrapped around him.

The Principle of Serving

Now that I, your Lord and Teacher, have washed your feet, you also should wash one another's feet. **I have set you an example that you should do as I have done for you.** *Very truly I tell you, no servant is greater than his master, nor is a messenger greater than the one who sent him.*

Jesus shows compassion when he told the disciples not to send the people away but feed them when he multiplied the boy's 2 pieces of fish and 5 loaves of bread: **John 6:5-6 & 9-13.**

Lifting up his eyes, then, and seeing that a large crowd was coming toward him, Jesus said to Philip, "Where are we to buy bread, so that these people may eat? He said this to test him, for He himself knew what he would do. There is a boy here who has five barley loaves and two fish, but what are they for so many? **Jesus said, "have the people sit down." So the men sat down, about five thousand in number. Jesus then took the loaves, and when he had given thanks, he distributed them to those who were seated.** *So also the fish, as much as they wanted. And when they had eaten their fill, he told his disciples, "gather up the leftover fragments, that nothing may be lost."*

CHOSEN

So they gathered them up and filled twelve baskets with fragments from the five barley loaves left by those who had eaten (John 6:5-6 & 9-13), ESV.

Jesus shows the Widow Woman compassion when He rebukes death and returns the man to his mother, during the funeral procession:

Luke 7:11-15. *And it came to pass the day after, that he went into a city called Nain; and many of his disciples went with him, and much people. Now when he came nigh to the gate of the city, behold, there was a dead man carried out, the only son of his mother, and she was a widow; and much people of the city was with her.* **And when the Lord saw her, He had compassion on her, and said unto her, Weep not.** *And He came and touched the bier: and they that bare him stood still. And He said, Young man, I say unto thee, Arise. And he that was dead sat up, and began to speak. And He delivered him to his mother.*

The Principle of Serving

Jesus serves and heals as a loving father before his arrest, he restores one of the servant ears when Peter cut it off: **Luke 22:50-51.**

And one of them smote the servant of the high priest, and cut off his right ear. And Jesus answered and said, suffer ye thus far. ***And he touched his ear; and healed him.***

Jesus asks His father to forgive those who crucified him, (love your enemies): **Luke 23:33-34.**

And there were also two other, malefactors, led with him to be put to death. And when they were come to the place, which is called Calvary, there they crucified him, and the malefactors, one on the right hand, and the other on the left. Then said Jesus, ***Father, forgive them; for they know not what they do.*** *And they parted his raiment, and cast lots.*

Serving in Ministry

Serving or having a servant's heart is essential to what God requires of you if you love Him (there's no need to feel pressured or forced to serve in ministry).

CHOSEN

Once you have given your heart to Jesus and begin to grow in your faith, your love and in the Word, you will eventually sense the leading of your talents and spiritual gifts; then you can freely pursue those ministries (I Corth. 12:4-7). Your servitude towards others and putting your fellow sisters and brothers needs before yours has promoted you to the front of the line. When you take care of God's business first, He takes care of yours. Promotions are on the way!

> *Serving in ministry also brings about spiritual growth for you and for others.*

Someone who may desire to serve in ministry may be somewhat fearful to take the step of faith and lead in their spiritual talents or gifts. Your faithful service in the ministry that they witness will encourage them and help them gain confidence that they too can move forward in servanthood.

The Principle of Serving

Even the Old Testament characters served in their roles of kingship or leadership. Your love, humility, faith and having the right spirit will help you in becoming a servant.

But what about those people who doesn't have a servant's heart but may be interested in serving?

If you desire to serve, there are several ways to serve others if you are not a Christian. You can start with your immediate family and serve them, not as being a slave but ensuring all of their well-being needs and happiness are met to the best of your ability. You can even serve in your community, a nonprofit organization or at your workplace.

As each has received a gift, use it to serve one another, as good stewards of God's varied grace; whoever speaks, as one who speaks oracles of God; whoever serves, as one who serves by the strength that God supplies, in order that in everything God may be glorified through Jesus Christ. To him belong glory and dominion forever and ever (I Peter 4:10-11), esv.

CHOSEN

Defining your Servanthood gifts:

On the lines provided here, consider a ministry in your church, a department at your workplace, or ... an organization in your community where you can serve.

_____

_____

_____

_____

_____

The Principle of Serving

Points to review for the Serving Principle

- *Jesus is our defining example of having a servant's heart and servanthood.*

- *Having a servant's heart has nothing to do with pleasing yourself, but how you can make a situation better for another or others.*

- *Characteristics of a servant's heart includes, but not limited to: disciplined, loving, faithful, kind, humble, honest, mature, forgiving, longsuffering, etc.*

- *Having the right spirit or a good attitude is always important when serving.*

- *Jesus maintained focus doing His Father's will and serving others, even during the crucifixion on the cross.*

- *Servitude assures promotions when you take care of God's business first.*

Chapter 7

The Principle of IDENTITY

The Road to Damascus

Bible Characters Identity

Defining your Identity

The Prodigal Son

Guard & Protect your Identity

Sunday School Trivia

Reflections Activity

Review

Identity

Before I formed you in the womb I knew and approved of you (as my chosen instrument), and before you were born I separated and set you apart, consecrating you; I appointed you as a prophet to the nations (Jer. 1:5), amp.

"The fact of being who or what a person or thing is; a close similarity or affinity; the distinguishing character or personality of an individual," (Merriam-Webster.com / Dictionary.com)."

The *Identity Principle* was *chosen* to be at the *"end"* of this writing, instead of the 1st chapter because most people remember what they read last. Some people like to go to the last chapter of a book or read the summary to see if it catches their attention.

Throughout the Old Testament we see how the Children of Israel had experienced many hardships and discouragements. They worshipped a false god, murmured and complained against God and His *chosen* leaders.

CHOSEN

And they had soon forgotten all that God had done for them.

But in spite of all that the Children of Israel had done and endured, they were still known as, "God's **Chosen** People," and they were still destined for the Promised Land.

God continued to provide for the children of Israel and He showed them signs, wonders, and many miracles during their wilderness experience.

Does any of the Children of Israel behaviors remind you of anyone you know?

The Bible Character's *Identity* was significant in many ways. Some of their names were given according to the situation surrounding their birth. And, many of their identity foretold their kingship which was prophesied before their birth; their names identified that they were *chosen* and special to God.

We see that some of the characters names were also changed to signify that a miracle had happened to them and God was about to do something different with them and in their future.

The Road to Damascus: Acts 9:1-19

Saul in the New Testament name was also changed to Paul when he was struck down on the road to Damascus for persecuting Christians. Once your name was changed by the Most High God, we see that person lived and reigned according to God's plan for their life. They were no longer identified by their previous name. Paul continued serving, writing and saving souls for the kingdom of God after his conversion and name change.

Many of the Bible Characters that God used, they all had some sort of problem that they had to overcome. Many of them felt that they were not smart enough, not eloquent enough, not old enough or even not capable enough to be used by the Lord.

CHOSEN

Well-known Bible Characters and their Identity

Abraham & Sarah: The father of many nations, a friend of God, the promised child when they had passed child bearing age.
Jacob: Trickster, fought with an Angel, God later changed his name to Israel.
Moses: Drawn out of the river by Pharaoh's daughter, the parting of the red sea and led the children of Israel across the red sea.
Enoch: Man of faith and obedient, he did not experienced death.
David: Danced before the Lord, a heart to please God, slued Goliath.
Samuel: Called by God as a child, young King.
Samson: Lost his vision and hair by confiding in Delilah.
Elijah: God's prophet, performed many miracles.
Ester: Queen appointed to King Ahasuerus, she replaced Queen Vashti.

Jonah: In the belly of the whale, disobeyed God's command.

Jeremiah: Emotional, young prophet.

Boaz: A wealthy landowner marries Ruth.

Elizabeth: Mother of John the Baptist; he prepared the way for Jesus.

Paul & Silas: Supernaturally released from Roman Jail by signing and praying.

Zacchaeus: Short in statue, climbed a tree to see Jesus.

Judas: Betrayed Jesus for 30 pieces of silver during the crucifixion.

Peter: Walked on water and denied Jesus 3 times.

Thomas: Known as doubting Thomas.

Defining your Identity

"Where are you?" Gen. 3:9 ………

This question was asked of Adam when he and Eve ate from the tree (the knowledge of good and evil) that God told them not to touch.

That question may seem confusing to the reader since God is all knowing and all seeing (Psa. 139:7- 8, Prov. 15:3).

Why did God ask Adam where are you? You must know that our disobedience will often be in question as we follow Christ on the righteous path.

God will call to us and seek us out, so we can remember who we are and where we are when we have fallen short of His grace. God can give us the ultimate punishment and send us straight to hell but his love, grace and mercy restores us.

God wants you to humbly acknowledge and confess your sins that He can put you back on the right path to get all that He has for you. If we choose not to humble ourselves and repent of our sins then we could possibly find ourselves in several situations heading in the opposite direction (Tarshish) as Jonah did (Jonah 1:17) and/or blinded and shaven like Samson.

But Jonah repented and had another opportunity to do what God had commanded of him. The whale spewed Jonah out right where he needed to be in Nineveh after being in the whale for three days and three nights.

Then Jonah decided to humble himself and he repented. And Samson hair started to grow back upon his repentance of bad choices and disobedience (Judg. 16:21-22).

"What is your name?" Mark 5:9 ......
Jesus asked the man who lived in the tomb that was tormented by an unclean spirit; the man was bound by shackles and chains and he was cutting himself with stones. Jesus already knew the man's name, right, but why did He ask him his name?

I believe Jesus wanted the man to identify the thing that kept him bound. The man replied, "my name is legion, for we are many."

Jesus wanted the man to remember his first identity and that he didn't have to be bound by what caused him to live like this. Once the man said that his name was legion being many, God was able to set the man free.

We see in verses, 18 & 19 of this story that the freed man wanted to go with Jesus. But Jesus refused to permit him, but told the man, **"go home to your family and relatives and tell them how much Jesus had done for you."** I believe what Jesus told the freed man is also a message for you and me.

Our true identity can only be found in Christ, but we have to first identify those chains that have stolen our identity and bound us. Those chains and bondage have caused us to act out of our true character. Only then we can become free to serve and have a relationship with our Father. We will be able to share with our family and others what Jesus has done in our lives, just as Jesus told the freed man.

The Principle of Identity

And the Lord said, "Simon, Simon! Indeed, satan has asked for you, that he may sift you as wheat. But I have prayed for you, that your faith should not fail; and when you have returned to Me, strengthen your brethren" (Luke 22:31-32), lab.

Jabez ...... in the Old Testament received his name by his mother birthing him in sorrow and in pain when he was born. This is where we learned about, "the prayer of Jabez."

And Jabez called on the God of Israel saying, "Oh, that you would bless me indeed, and enlarge my territory, that you would be with me, and that You would keep me for evil, that I may not cause pain!" So God granted him what he requested (I Chron. 4:10), nkjv.

The Parable of the Prodigal Son: Luke 15:11-24:
And He said, A certain man had two sons: And the younger of them said to his father, "Father, give me the portion of goods that falls to me."

And he divided to them his living. And not many days after, the younger son gathered all together, and he took his journey into a far county, and there he wasted his substance with riotous living."

Verse 17:
But when he came to himself, he said, how many hired servants of my father have bread enough and to spare, and I perish with hunger!"

Verse 21:
And the son said to him, Father, I have sinned against heaven and in your sight, and am no more worthy to be called your son.

Verse 24:
For this my son was dead and is alive again; he was lost and is found. And they began to be merry.

In the Prodigal Son story, the younger son thought that he could do better being disconnected from his father. When he came to himself, or ...... when he humbled himself and remembered all that he already had being connected to his father, (he didn't have

The Principle of Identity

to continue eating with the pigs because God already had the best for him).
The father didn't have his servants to send his son away when he saw him coming for all that he had done, but rather, the father loved him and showed his son compassion.

The father received his son with open arms, a kiss, a ring, shoes and a party! This is a wonderful story to remind all of us how our heavenly father calls to us when we go astray. He seeks us and He shows us compassion when we repent, and humble ourselves and return to Him. The son's true identity was seen in this story as being connected to his father.

Guard & Protect your Identity

The 7 principles in obtaining your destiny are equally important but the *identity principle* should help you to remember who you are in Christ first.
There will be many people and several things on our *chosen* path that we will attach

ourselves to and lose focus of our priority and Identity. This can cause us to become derailed also, if you are not discerning the right spirit. It may be a spirit, but is it the right spirit?

I will use our famous quote here, **"the-devil-made- me-do-it."** But to be honest, we did it ourselves, and we wanted to do it. There are many times when the tempter will spread it on real thick and plant the wrong thoughts in your mind. The phrase I often hear since my circle of influence involves people of all ages and from various socioeconomic groups, they would often say, "I didn't expect this or that to happen."

These mishaps usually takes you by surprise when you didn't get enough information or education about something the enemy has lowered you into. Before you know it, you're hooked (add your vices here) or, you got something that you didn't planned for, and "that thing" just lingers on.

There WILL be traps and/or detours on your path that can hold you captive.

Don't allow --- your heart, your emotions, your feelings and your integrity to get torn-up and smeared by something/someone that you didn't check out first. The Christian community would say, "C-h-i-l-d, you should pray about that or give it some time to understand, who/what you are dealing with." But, that might be a difficult thing for you to do if you're not practicing mature faith.

We all have sinned and made mistakes, and remember the single track that keeps you isolated and going no-where is not worth losing all that God has predestined for you (James 1:12-16).

CHOSEN

The Identity Principle shapes your purpose and value of which we are called by God:

> Royal
> Special
> **Chosen**
> Jewels
> Beloved
> Precious
> A Sweet Savor
> Valued Treasures
> Apple of His eyes
> Head and not the tail
> Lender and not a borrower
> Fearfully and wonderfully made

My point is your Identity is so very important to God because we were purchased with a high price. Your identity should be guarded and protected that you can show forth all of God's blessings and splendor, now that you have been *chosen* by Him!

Sunday School Trivia:

In the following section, name the Bible Characters you remember from Sunday school; if you did not attend Sunday school then this would be a good opportunity for you to search the scriptures.

God told this man to build an Ark. The ark was three hundred cubits long, fifty cubits wide and thirty cubits high.
Bible Character's Name: _____, & Scripture: _____.

This woman "name" was different; she hid her baby for 3 months; she had put her baby in a basket in the Nile River so her baby boy wouldn't be killed.
Bible Character's Name: _____, & Scripture: _____.

This young man was loved especially by his father, Jacob. He had a dream that his brothers would bow down to him.
Bible Character' Name: _____, & Scripture: _____.

CHOSEN

This woman was called "barren." She prayed for God to bless her with a son; her husband's name was Elkanah.
Bible Character's Name: _____, &
Scripture: _____

This young man wanted to have a double portion of his mentor's anointing. His mentor said, you have asked a hard thing.
Bible Character's Name: _____, &
Scripture: _____.

This woman was known for having a condition for 12 years, and she was healed when she touched Jesus garment as He was passing by.
Bible Character's Name: _____, &
Scripture: _____.

This man was known to receive double from the Lord during his latter years because he had lost everything: his wealth, his health and his children; The Lord blessed his latter days more than his beginning.
Bible Character's Name: _____, &
Scripture: _____.

The Principle of Identity

This faithful man was first introduced in the faith by his Mother Eunice and Grandmother Lois.
Bible Character's Name: _____, & Scripture: _____.

Reflections

We see in the *Identity* Chapter that the Bible Characters names meant great significance during that person's birth, and some of their names were changed for something that God was doing with them and for their future.

God used several ways to remind them of their true identity. He would call to them or even ask their name for them to remember who they are and not for the thing that was currently plaguing or bounding them.

God uses love, humility, compassion, and grace as He restores His children and put us back on the righteous path.

CHOSEN

He calls us *"CHOSEN"* because we were made in His image, and for his unconditional love and mercy towards us, and also for his desire to bless us!

God shows His unconditional love when He go after one lost soul or sheep (Matt. 18:12 & Luke 15:4) until he gets you back in the fold. He said that no one can pluck you out of his hand (John 10:28).

God has already *chosen* a great destiny for you before you knew it. All of His blessings are, **"Yes and Amen."** We can be honest with ourselves and identify those things that keep us bound from moving forward. Once you identify it, only then you can receive freedom and restoration.

Blessed and worthy of praise be the God and Father of our Lord Jesus Christ, who has blessed us with every spiritual blessing in the heavenly realms in Christ, just as He chose us in Christ before the foundation of the world, so that we would be holy and blameless in His sight. In love He predestined and lovingly planned

The Principle of Identity

for us to be adopted to Himself as His own children through Jesus Christ, in accordance with the kind intention and good pleasure of his will (Ephes. 1:3-5), amp.

***NOW* ...** is the time for you to dust off and complete those projects you have put on hold or laid on the shelf. Once you get started you will be amazed at all the creative ideas inside of you. Your expertise, your skills, your trade, your convictions, your personality, your culture, etc.... have afforded you to succeed; you have all you need already.

These 7 principles were designed to guide and navigate you through your destiny journey, and to keep you on the righteous path. The amazing thing about these principles are, you may already have them in your life and they are practical enough for you to remember. The activities will also help you to stay focused on your own *chosen* path, **share them with a friend.**

> *God will make your name great,*
> *and bring you before great men.*
> *Envision yourself now, achieving all*
> *that God has for you and strolling*
> *along the red carpet !*

The red-carpet scene is not just for "Hollywood Celebrities or the rich and famous," but also for those who dare to trust God. There are many promises in store for us but we have to take hold of them by **FAITH**. It will only happen when you take the 1st step of faith .... just as I did with completing this book (Gen. 12:2 & Prov. 18:16).

And I didn't find this assignment difficult at all; it only took my faith to the next level. My desire is to be willing and obedient.

No more negotiating and bargaining with the devil; you are God's original and not a cheap second hand copy. There's a great destiny *chosen* for you and you can't allow anything to cripple your true identity from what God has purposed for you.

The Principle of Identity

The devil will try to fool you and throw distractions in your path. And you may even witness with your own eyes fierce weapons that are formed against you, **BUT IT WON'T PROSPER!!** Never settle for anything that's less than God's best. You can have what God said belongs to you!

By having the eyes of your heart flooded with light, so that you can know and understand the hope to which He has called you, and how rich is His glorious inheritance in the saints. His set apart ones (Eph. 1:18), amp.

As we see in the scriptures, God won't allow you to venture off to far from the *chosen* path before He returns you to the fold. You already know the devil schemes and tricks by now; you've wasted enough time in Lodebar, let's go eat at the **KING'S TABLE!!**

CHOSEN

Reflect here .....

On the lines provided here, identify, "that thing," or "the chains," that's keeping you bound from true freedom or from you moving forward on the righteous path.

_____

_____

_____

_____

_____

The Principle of Identity

Points to review for the Identity Principle

- ✓ *In spite of the Children of Israel's hardships and murmuring they were identified as God's **chosen** people.*

- ✓ *The Bible Character's Identity or names were predetermined for their kingship roles and their future ministry.*

- ✓ *Your identity has great significance when you remain connected to God, the true vine.*

- ✓ *You can pray and appeal to God to change your future path if there were negative connotation surrounding your birth.*

- ✓ *You were purchased with a high price to show forth the glory of God, therefore, guard and protect your identity.*

- ✓ *God will seek you and go after you if you lose your Identity and leave the fold.*

- ✓ *God can restore our true identity when we humbly repent and return to Him.*

Reviews

Chosen is an excellent resource for anyone seeking to become a faithful disciple of Jesus Christ. Cheryl has invited the reader to join her on a spiritual journey that revealed her love for the Lord. ***Chosen*** is an easy read; you will not want to put it down.
Thank you for allowing me to be one of the persons you invited to give a review for your first book. Again, I am so proud of you! Great Job!

Your Sister,

Rev. Connie Barnes
Senior Pastor
Rehoboth UM Church Columbia, SC

As I began to read and review simultaneously the Book, **"CHOSEN"** written by Cheryl Nelson, I realized very early on that Cheryl was destined from childhood to walk into her Royal Priesthood. She was truly *chosen* and equipped with the necessary tools to take this journey. One important tool given to Cheryl by God was her early foundation laid down from the ole-school which taught the teenagers in those days to "seek and tarry."
I believe this is where the Holy Spirit met her with open arms and began to help direct her path.

Other tools that Cheryl obtained along her journey was being a part of a prayer ministry as a young adult and also being given the task of helping with Vacation Bible School. This is where Cheryl became that Beautiful Butterfly and she began her cocoon process. She was gently transformed and learned to adhere to the sweet still voice of God. I also believe this is where she grew in strength as a single adult so that, she would not be easily distracted. Cheryl was able to gain momentum on her journey to achieve all that God intended for her life.

In Conclusion, It has been a pleasure to be *chosen* by Cheryl to offer my set of eyes for this review. I was able to be blessed as I read this book and, I was able to glean on this journey as we grew in a Spirit-filled Sisterhood for over twenty years. I am encouraged to continue on my journey with my necessary tools to finish this race. I am **Disciplined**, I will continue to **Persevere**, I will **Pray** without ceasing, my **Faith** is strengthened, daily I am **Humbled**, I love **Serving** others and my **Identity** was established in my mother's womb.

Blessings My Sister,
JoEllen Logan-McGee
Certified Nursing Assistant
Charleston, SC

CHOSEN

In Cheryl's Book *Chosen,* the reader will get great practical application and insights of the seven principles. Cheryl's use of the activities throughout the entire book will engage the reader to fully grasp these principles. Personally, I identified with the growth process in several chapters especially when Cheryl shares her testimonies. Trust in and rely confidently on the Lord with all your heart; and do not rely on your own insight or understanding. In all your ways know and acknowledge and recognize Him and He will make your paths straight and smooth (removing obstacles that block your way) Prov. 3:5-6, AMP. At the completion of reading this book, it's very obvious that Cheryl stood on this scripture (Prov. 3: 5-6) also, in order for her to achieve one of her goals for this awesome assignment.

May God Bless you mightily and those who read this book!

Deanna Hunt, Ed.D.
Special Education Teacher
Jonesboro, GA

Cheryl embraces a disciplined life by acknowledging God in everything she does. She touches the heart of God though prayer, worship, personal study, and fellowship. Cheryl's book, "**CHOSEN**," displays her testimony of God's Love. You will laugh and cry at how God showed His love towards her. He died, and lives for all, because you are *chosen.*

Reviews

As an author, Cheryl gives fulfilled hope and she speaks wisdom to her readers while instilling and empowering them to a path that will lead them to their destiny. As this book relates to me, I know how my destiny is to be fulfilled. You must stay connected to the Father, and you cannot beat the devil in your own strength. Now I do not have to continue going in circles and miss out getting on to the next track that will lead me to my Destiny.

It was awesome to read that I was not a mistake being born for a purpose, and my grand entrance was *chosen* for the life He planned for me. You will have hope for your Destiny as you download these principles of HIS love.

To my friend,

Deborah J. Arnold, Author
"Don't Let the Stranger In"
Community Activist
Atlanta, GA

About the Author

Chery was born in the small town of Bonneau, SC to Mary McKnight-Nelson and the late Joseph Nelson. Cheryl is the fifth child of ten siblings, and the youngest two sisters are twins.

The City of Bonneau or, "41 Community" and the City of St. Stephen are adjacent; they both are very small in population. If you have not heard of Bonneau then you may have heard of St. Stephen. And, if you have not heard of St. Stephen I'm sure you have heard of Charleston, SC. Bonneau is about 30 miles from the City of Charleston. Can anything good come out of Bonneau?

Cheryl has always known from a young child that there was something different that God was doing in her life. Cheryl's siblings would often say, "she think she's all that." Even her Mother Mary, family members, and friends would often jokingly say, **"She always had to have the best."**

Cheryl's Mother would say, she would wash the older sister's hand-me-downs and even tried to remake one of the sister's dresses or skirts to fit Cheryl, but she would never wear them. Cheryl recalled that the family would make fun of her about what Mom had said about her, even her four older siblings would add their two cents, and embellish what Mom said

About the Author

about her. Cheryl had to deal with the family's ridicules, and jokes, so, she just had to get over it until she finally accepted the fact that she was *"chosen,"* even as a kid!!

Cheryl and her siblings are a very humorous bunch as they can easily entertain each other when they get together. But on the other hand, it could be just the opposite! They do get on each other's nerves sometimes! There are ten different personalities in her family..... nine of them being women, and a, "one man show," a force to be reckoned with. If you happened to come against one of the siblings, "LOOK-OUT" you would have the **NEL10** on your backside.

Cheryl's parents and family used to shop at the famous, "5-&-Dime Store," when they were growing up. Her Mother Mary said that after she had made a purchase for Cheryl and if it didn't suit her fancy, Cheryl would say, "I don't want that," or "I'm not wearing that!"

The "5-&-Dime Store" was one of those stores that you could have purchased anything from: food, clothing, toiletries, school supplies, linens, shoes, furniture, etc. You name it, they had it. The "5-&-Dime Store" is probably considered like the Walmart Stores now.

CHOSEN

The family didn't have much as the children were growing up, but they were happy and they never went hungry. Cheryl's Mother Mary would always remind her children that they can't manage $50,000 a year's salary --- when her and her husband only had about $10,000 to $15,000 a year to live on. Mother Mary would often say, "I don't know how we did it, but we made it just fine and all our bills got paid."

Cheryl is a single woman who has hopes of promoting her business in various states and abroad. Her business will support women and non-traditional students with educational and GED resources, child care and transportation that they will become productive and self-sufficient. One of Cheryl's mottos is, "higher education is essential and invaluable for achieving some of your personal goals."

Cheryl received a Bachelor of Science Degree in Psychology and a Minor in Management from Georgia State University. Cheryl was inspired to pursue her master's degree in her *chosen* field after working in the admissions office and recruiting MBA prospectus students at Emory University. Several years later, Cheryl received her Masters of Education Degree in Mental Health Counseling from Cambridge College in Cambridge, Massachusetts.

Footnotes / References / Websites

Chapter 4: The Principle of Faith:
Weich, Susan. (2015, January). "Boy who fell through ice at Lake Sainte Louise." St. Louis Post-Dispatch, pg. A3.

Bible References & Versions used:

AMP   *Amplified Bible*   2015
The Lockman Foundation, La Habra, CA 90631

ERV   *English Revised Version*   1881-1985
C. J. Clay and Son, Cambridge Warehouse: Aye Maria Lane, London Oxford Warehouse: Amen Corner, London

ESV   *English Standard Version*   2001, 2007
Good News Publishers, Crossway Bibles, 8.0, 2011, 2016

ISV   *International Standard Version*
                                          1995-2014
Davidson Press, LLC. 2.1, The ISV Foundation 2011.

KJV   *King James Version*   1798
Thomas Nelson Publisher. Nashville, Tennessee, 37214 and Hendrickson Publishers. Peabody, Massachusetts, USA

LAB   *Life Application Bible*   1991
Tyndale House Publishers

NASB   New American Standard Bible
                                    1963, 1971
Reuben A. Olsen, et, al., Pilot, ed, La Habra, CA
                                    1995, 1999
Foundation Publication, The Lockman Foundation
                                    2015

NIV   New International Version, 1984, 2011
Zondervan Publishers in United States, and Hodder
& Stoughton in UK.   1973, 1978

NKJV   New King James Version   1982
Thomas Nelson Publisher

NLT   New Living Translation   1996, 2004,
                                    2007
Tyndale House Publishers, Inc. Carol Stream,
Illinois 60188.   2013, 2015

Website References:

https://www.BibleGateway.com
https://www.BibleHub.com
https://www. Christinity.com
www.Christianity.Stackexchange.com
https://www.Dictionary.com
https://www.Merriam-Webster.com
https://www.Netfind.com
https://www.Vocabulary.com

ST. LOUIS POST-DISPATCH

900 N. Tucker Blvd. St. Louis, MO 63101
o. 314-340-8102 | c. 314-456-1320 | f. 314-340-3095
mtomczak@post-dispatch.com

@stltoday

Cheryl,

Your due diligence has finally paid off!

You have our permission to reference the article on **John Smith** that appeared in the St. Louis Post-Dispatch on pg. A3 of the Jan. 21, 2015 print edition in your soon-to-be-published book titled:

CHOSEN, Principles for achieving your DESTINY.

Your footnoted credit should read: "As published in the St. Louis Post-Dispatch. 1-21-15; Story and photo by Susan Weich"

Our typical copyright fee has been waived.

We wish you success.

Regards,

Maureen Tomczak
Newsroom Administrative Assistant

Book Cover Art
& Memorial Flower Design
by:

scot mmobuosi
graphic artist / web designer

(914) 714 0027
scot@scotdesigns.com
www.scotdesigns.com

Back Cover Photo by:

Scripture References

Chapter 1: The Principle of Discipline
But seek aim at and strive after, 1st of all his kingdom and his righteous (His way of doing and being right) and then all of these things taken together will be given you (Matt. 6:33), amp.

Every scripture is God breathed and profitable for instruction, for reproof and conviction of sin, for correction of error and discipline in obedience for training in righteousness (in holy living, in conformity to God's will in thought, purpose, and action). So that the man of God may be complete and proficient, well fitted and thoroughly equipped for every good work (II Tim. 3:16-17), amp.

For the commandment is a lamp, and the teaching is light; and reproofs for discipline are the way of life (Prov. 6:23), nas.

Therefore, if anyone is in Christ, he is a new creation. The old has passed away; behold, the new has come (2 Corth. 5:17), nkjv.

If you remain in me and I in you, you will bear much fruit, Apart from me you can do nothing (John 15:5), nkjv.

Then Nebuchadnezzar said to them, is it true, O Shadrach, Meshach, and Abednego, that you do not serve my gods or worship the golden image which I have set up? Now if you are ready when you hear the sound of the horn, pipe, lyre, trigon, harp, dulcimer or bagpipe, and every kind of music to fall down and worship the image which I have made, very good. But if you do not worship, you shall be cast at once into the midst of a burning fiery furnace, and who is that god who can deliver you out of my hands? Then Nebuchadnezzar was full of fury and his facial expression was changed to antagonism against Shadrach, Meshach, and Abednego. Therefore he commanded that the furnace should be heated seven times hotter than it was usually heated. He answered, Behold, I see four men loose, walking in the midst of the fire, and they are not hurt! And the form of the fourth is like a son of the gods! And the satraps, the deputies, the governors, and the king's counselors gathered around together and saw these men – that the fire had no power upon their bodies, nor was the hair of their head singed; neither were their garments scorched or changed in color or condition, nor had even the smell of smoke clung to them. Then the king promoted Shadrach, Meshach, and Abednego in the province of Babylon (Daniel 3:14-15, 19, 25, 27, 30), amp.

Call on Me in the day of trouble; I will rescue you, and you shall honor and glorify Me (Psa. 50:15), niv.

If you live in me (abide vitally united to me) and My words remain in you and continue to live in your hearts, ask whatever you will and it shall be done for you (Jn. 15:5), amp.

Chapter 2: The Principle of Perseverance

Not that I have already attained, or am already perfected; but I press on that I may lay hold of that for which Christ Jesus has also laid hold of me (Phil: 3-12), nkjv.

Weeping may endure for a night, but joy cometh in the morning (Psa. 30:5), amp.

You have not chosen Me, but I have chosen you and I have appointed and placed and purposefully planted you, so that you would go and bear fruit and keep on bearing, and that your fruit will remain and be lasting, so that whatever you ask of the Father in My name He may give to you (John 15:16), amp.

There was a judge in a certain city, he said, who neither feared God nor cared about people. A widow of that city came to him repeatedly, saying, give me justice in this dispute with my enemy. The judge ignored her for a while, but finally he said to himself, I don't fear God or care about people, but this woman is driving me crazy. I'm going to see that she gets justice, because she is wearing me out with her constant requests! Then the

Lord said, "Learn a lesson from this unjust judge." Even he rendered a just decision in the end. So, don't you think God will surely give justice to his chosen people who cry out to him day and night? Will he keep putting them off? I tell you, he will grant justice to them quickly! (Luke 18:2-8), nlt.

The word which came to Jeremiah from the Lord, saying; Arise and go down to the potter's house, and there I will cause you to hear My words. Then I went down to the potter's house, and there he was, making something at the wheel. And the vessel that he made of clay was marred in the hand of the potter; so he made it again into another vessel, as it seemed good to the potter to make (Jere. 18:1-4), nkjv.

Let us not become weary in doing good, for at the proper time we will reap a harvest if we do not give up (Gal. 6:9), niv.

For the weapons of our warfare are not carnal, but mighty through God to the pulling down of strong holds (II Corint. 10:4), kjv.

Tomorrow go ye down against them; behold, they come up by the cliff of Ziz; and ye shall find them at the end of the brook, before the wilderness of Jeruel. Ye shall not need to fight in this battle: set yourselves, stand ye still, and see the salvation of the Lord with you, O Judah and Jerusalem: fear not, nor be dismayed;

tomorrow go out against them: for the Lord will be with you (II Chron. 20:16-17), kjv.

I will say of the LORD, He is my refuge and my fortress, my God, in whom I trust (Psa. 91:2), niv.

Chapter 3: The Principle of Prayer
The effective, fervent prayers of a righteous man avails much (b), (James 5:16), nkjv.

And David inquired of the Lord, saying, Shall I pursue this troop? Shall I overtake them? The Lord answered him, Pursue, for you shall surely overtake them and without fail recover all. David recovered all that the Amalekites had taken and secured his two wives. Nothing was missing, small or great, sons or daughters, spoil or anything that had been taken; David recovered all (I Samuel 30:8, 18-19), amp.

At the time of the offering of the evening sacrifice, Elijah the prophet came near and said, O Lord, the God of Abraham, Isaac, and Israel, let it be known this day that you are God in Israel and that I am Your servant and that I have done all these things at your word. Hear me, O Lord, hear me, that this people may know that you, the Lord are God, and have turned their hearts back to you. Then the fire of the Lord fell and consumed the burnt sacrifice and the wood and the stones and the dust, and also licked up the water that was in the trench. When all the people saw it, they fell on their faces and they said, The Lord He is God! The Lord, He is God ! (I Kings 18:36-39), nasb.

In those days Hezekiah became deadly ill. The prophet Isaiah son of Amoz came and said to him Thus says the Lord: Set your house in order, for you shall die; you shall not recover. Then Hezekiah turned his face to the wall and prayed to the Lord, saying, I beseech You, O Lord, earnestly remember now how I have walked before You in faithfulness and truth and with a whole heart entirely devoted to You, and have done what is good in Your sight. And Hezekiah wept bitterly. Before Isaiah had gone out of the Middle court, the word for the Lord came to him: Turn back and tell Hezekiah, the leader of my people, Thus says the Lord, the God of David your (forefather): I have heard your prayer, I have seen your tears; behold, I will heal you. On the third day you shall go up to the house of the Lord (II Kings 20:1-5), amp.

And Hannah was in distress of soul, praying to the Lord and weeping bitterly. She vowed, saying, O lord of hosts, if You will indeed look on the affliction of Your handmaid and earnestly remember, and not forget your handmaid but will give me a son, I will give him to the Lord all his life no razor shall touch his head. And as she continued praying before the Lord, Eli noticed her mouth. Hannah was speaking in her heart; only her lips moved but her voice was not heard.

So Eli thought she was drunk. Eli said to her, how long will you be intoxicated? Put wine away from you. But Hannah answered, No, my Lord, I am a woman of a sorrowful spirit. I have drunk neither wine nor strong drink, but I was pouring out my soul before the Lord. Regard not your handmaid as a wicked woman; for out of my great complaint and bitter provocation I have been speaking. Then Eli said, Go in peace, and may the God of Israel grant your petition which you have asked of Him. Hannah became pregnant and in due time bore a son and named him Samuel (heard of God), because, she said, I have asked him of the Lord (I Samuel 1:10-17 & 20), amp.

But about midnight, as Paul and Silas were praying and singing hymns of praise to God, and the other prisoners were listening to them. Suddenly there was a great earthquake, so that the very foundations of the prison were shaken; and at once all the doors were opened and everyone's shackles were unfastened (Acts 16:25-26), amp.

By this My Father is glorified, that you bear much fruit; so you will be my disciples. You did not choose Me, but I chose you and appointed you that you should go and bear fruit, band that your fruit should remain, that whatever you ask the Father in My name He may give you (Jn. 15:8 & 16), nkjv.

For God so greatly loved and dearly prized the world that He gave up His only begotten son, so that whoever believes in (trusts in, clings to, relies on) Him shall not perish, come to destruction or lost but have eternal everlasting life (John 3:16), amp.

Because if you acknowledge and confess with your mouth that Jesus is Lord and believe in your heart (adhere to, trust in, and rely on the truth) that God raised Jesus from the dead, you will be saved. For with the heart a person believes and so is justified and with the mouth the confession of salvation (Rom. 10:9-10), amp.

Like newborn infants, long for the pure spiritual milk, that by it you may grow up into salvation (I Peter 2:2), esv.

Likewise, I say to you, there is joy in the presence of the angels of God over one sinner who repents (Luke 15:10), nkjv.

And you are complete in him, who is the head of all principality and power (Col. 2:10), nkjv.

Chapter 4: The Principle of Faith

Now faith is the substance of things hoped for, the evidence of things not seen (Heb. 11:1), nkjv.

And it is impossible to please God without faith. Anyone who wants to comes to Him must believe that God exists and that he rewards those who sincerely seek Him (Heb. 11:6), nlt.

For we are God's own handiwork, his workmanship, recreated in Christ Jesus, born anew that we may do those good works which God predestined (planned beforehand) for us taking paths which He prepared ahead of time, that we should walk in them, living the good life which He prearranged and made ready for us to live (Eph. 2:10), amp.

And we know that all things work together for good to them that love God, to them who ae called according to his purpose (Rom. 8:28), kjv.

People might make many plans, but what the Lord says is what will happen (Prov. 19:21), erv.

For I know the plans I have for you, declares the LORD, plans to prosper you and not to harm you, plans to give you hope and a future (Jer. 29:11), niv.

Submit yourself therefore to God. Resist the devil, and he will flee from you (James 4:7), kjv.

The thief comes only in order to steal and kill and destroy. I came that they may have and enjoy life, and have it in abundance, to the full, till it overflows (John 10:10), amp.

Be diligent to present yourself approved to God, a worker who does not need to be ashamed, rightly dividing the word of truth (II Timothy 2:15), nkjv.

For the weapons of our warfare are not carnal, flesh, but mighty through God to the pulling down of strong holds (II Corth. 10:4), kjv.

When Jesus had entered Capernaum, a centurion came to him, asking for help. "Lord," he said, "my servant lies at home paralyzed, suffering terribly." Jesus said to him, "Shall I come and heal him ?" The Centurion replied, "Lord, I do not deserve to have you come under my roof. But just say the word, and my servant will be healed. For I myself am a man under authority, with soldiers under me. I tell this one, "go," and he goes; and that one, "come," and he comes. I say to my servant, "do this,"and he does it." When Jesus heard this, He was amazed and said to those following him, "Truly I tell you, I have not found anyone in Israel with such great faith. Then Jesus said to the centurion, "Go! Let it be done just as you believed it would." And his servant was healed at that moment (Matt. 8:5-10 & 13), niv.

And Jesus said to him, "Go your way; "your faith has mad you well." And immediately he recovered his sight and followed him on the way (Mark 10:52), esv.

Fear not, for I am with you; be not dismayed, for I am your God; I will strengthen you, I will help you, I will uphold you with my righteous right hand (Isa. 41:10), esv.

For God hath not given us the spirit of fear; but of power, and of love, and of a sound mind (II Tim. 1:7), kjv.

The Lord is my light and my salvation; whom shall I fear? The Lord is the strength of my life; of whom shall I be afraid? When the wicked, even mine enemies and my foes, came upon me to eat up my flesh, they stumbled and fell. Though an host should encamp against me, my heart shall not fear; though war should rise against me, in this will I be confident (Pas. 27:1-3), kjv.

For all the promises of God in Him are Yes, and in Him Amen, to the glory of God through us (II Corth. 1:20), nkjv.

For I will contend with him who contends with you, and I will save your children (Isa. 49:25-b), nkjv.

And they overcame him by the blood of the Lamb and by the word of their testimony (Rev. 12:11), nkjv.

Saying, if you will diligently hearken to the voice of the Lord your God and will do what is right in His sight, and will listen to and obey His commandments and keep all His statures, I will put none of the diseases upon you which I brought upon the Egyptians, for I am the Lord Who heals you (Exod. 15:26), amp.

Chapter 5: The Principle of Humility

Therefore humble yourself under the mighty hand of God, that he may exalt you in due time (1 Peter 5:6), nkjv.

You saw me before I was born. Every day of my life was recorded in your book. Every moment was laid out before a single day had passed (Psa. 139:16), nlt.

Therefore the Lord himself will give you a sign; The virgin will conceive and give birth to a son, and will call him Immanuel (Isa. 7:14), niv.

All this took place to fulfill what the Lord had said through the prophet: The virgin will conceive and give birth to a son, and they will call him Immanuel, which means God with us (Matt. 1:22-23), niv.

But when the set time had fully come, God sent his Son, born of a woman, born under the law, to redeem those under the law, that we might receive adoption to sonship (Gal 4:4-5), niv.

He was oppressed an afflicted, yet he did not open his mouth; he was led like a lamb to the slaughter, and as a sheep before its shearers is silent, so he did not open his mouth (Isa. 53:7), niv.

The angel said to the woman, "Do not be afraid, for I know that you are looking for Jesus, who was crucified. He is not here; he has risen, just as he said. Come and see the place here he lay (Matt. 28:5-6), niv.

And Joseph also went up from Galilee from the town of Nazareth to Judea, to the town of David, which is called Bethlehem, because he was of the house and family of David. To be enrolled with Mary, his espoused, married wife, who was about to become a mother. And while they were there, the time came for her delivery, and she gave birth to her Son, her Firstborn; and she wrapped Him in swaddling clothes and laid Him in a manger, because there was no room or place for them in the inn. And in that vicinity there were shepherds living out under the open sky in the field, watching in shifts over their flock by night. And behold, an angel of the Lord stood by them and the glory of the Lord flashed and shone all about them, and they were terribly frightened (Luke 2:4-9), amp.

He was despised and rejected and forsaken by men, a Man of sorrows and pains and acquainted with grief and sickness; and like One from Whom men hide their faces He was despised, and we did not appreciate His worth or have any esteem for Him (Isa. 53:3), amp.

I have been crucified with Christ and I no longer live, but Christ lives in me. The life I now live in the body, I live by faith in the Son of God, who loved me and gave himself for me (Gal. 2:20), niv.

He called a little child to him, and placed the child among them. And He said: Truly I tell you, unless you change and become like little children, you will never enter the kingdom of heaven. Therefore, whoever takes the lowly position of this child is the greatest in the kingdom of heaven, (Matt. 18:2-4), niv.

And he charged them that they should tell no man; but the more he charged them, so much the more a great deal they published it (Mark 7:36), erv.

If my people, which are called by my name, shall humble themselves, and pray, and seek my face, and turn from their wicked ways; then will I hear from heaven, and will forgive their sin, and will heal their land (2 Chron. 7:14), kjv.

A man's pride will bring him low: but honor shall uphold the humble in spirit (Pro. 29:23), kjv.

Let nothing be done through selfish ambition or conceit, but in lowliness of mind let each esteem others better than himself. Let each of you look out not only for his own interests, but also for the interests of others (Phil. 2:3-4), njkv.

Chapter 6: The Principle of Serving

For even the Son of Man came not to be served but to serve, and to give his life as a ransom for many (Mark 10:45), esv.

Whatever you do, work at it wholeheartedly as though you were doing it for the Lord and not merely for people, knowing that from the Lord you will receive the inheritance as your reward (Col 3:23-24), isv.

Jesus knew that the Father had put all things under his power, and that he had come from God and was returning to God: so he got up from the meal, took off his outer clothing, and wrapped a towel around his waist. After that, he poured water into a basin and began to wash his disciples' feet, drying them with the towel that was wrapped around him. Now that I, your Lord and Teacher, have washed your feet, you also should wash one another's feet. I have set you an example that you should do as I have done for you.
Very truly I tell you, no servant is greater than his master, nor is a messenger greater than the one who sent him (John 13:3-5 & 14-16), niv.

Lifting up his eyes, then, and seeing that a large crowd was coming toward him, Jesus said to Philip, "Where are we to buy bread, so that these people may eat ? He said this to test him, for he himself knew what he would do. There is a boy here who has five barley loaves and two fish, but what are they for so many ? Jesus said, "have the people sit down." So the men sat down, about five thousand in number. Jesus then took the loaves, and when he had given thanks, he distributed them to those who were seated. So also the fish, as much as they wanted. And when they had eaten their fill, he told his disciples, "gather up the leftover fragments, that nothing may be lost." So they gathered them up and filled twelve baskets with fragments from the five barley loaves left by those who had eaten (John 6:5-6 & 9-13), esv.

And it came to pass the day after, that he went into a city called Nain; and many of his disciples went with him, and much people. Now when he came nigh to the gate of the city, behold, there was a dead man carried out, the only son of his mother, and she was a widow; and much people of the city was with her. And when the Lord saw her, he had compassion on her, and said unto her, Weep not. And he came and touched the bier: and they that bare him stood still. And he said, Young man, I say unto thee, Arise. And he that was dead sat up, and began to speak. And he delivered him to his mother (Luke 7:11-15), kjv.

And one of them smote the servant of the high priest, and cut off his right ear. And Jesus answered and said, suffer ye thus far. And he touched his ear; and healed him (Luke 22:50-51), kjv.

And there were also two other, malefactors, led with him to be put to death. And when they were come to the place, which is called Calvary, there they crucified him, and the malefactors, one on the right hand, and the other on the left. Then said Jesus, Father, forgive them; for they know not what they do. And they parted his raiment, and cast lots (Luke 23:32-34), kjv.

There are different kinds of gifts, but the same Spirit distributes them. There are different kinds of service, but the same Lord. There are different kinds of working, but in all of them and in everyone it is the same God at work (I Corth. 12:4-7), niv.

As each has received a gift, use it to serve one another, as good stewards of God's varied grace; whoever speaks, as one who speaks oracles of God; whoever serves, as one who serves by the strength that God supplies, in order that in everything God may be glorified through Jesus Christ. To him belong glory and dominion forever and ever (I Peter 4:10-11), esv.

Chapter 7: The Principle of Identity

Before I formed you in the womb I knew and approved of you (as my chosen instrument), and before you were born I separated and set you apart, consecrating you; I appointed you as a prophet to the nations (Jer. 1:5), amp.

And as he journeyed, he came near Damascus and suddenly there shined round about him a light from heaven, and he fell to the earth, and heard a voice saying unto him, Saul, Saul, why persecutes thou me? And he said, Who art thou, Lord? And the Lord said, I am Jesus whom thou persecutest, it is hard for thee to kick against the pricks. And he trembling and astonished said, Lord what wilt thou have me to do? And the Lord said unto him, Arise and go into the city, and it shall be told thee what thou must do (Acts 9:1-6), nkjv.

And the Lord God called unto Adam, and said unto him, Where art thou? (Gen. 3:9), kjv.

Now the Lord had prepared a great fish to swallow up Johan. And Jonah was in the belly of the fish three days and three nights (Jonah 1:17), kjv.

Then the Philistines seized him, gouged out his eyes and took him down to Gaza. Binding him with bronze shackles, they set him to grinding grain in the prison.

But the hair on his head began to grow again after it had been shaved (Judg. 16:21-22), niv.

And Jesus asked him, "What is your name?" He replied, "My name is Legion, for we are many" (Mark 5:9), esv.

As Jesus was getting into the boat, the man who had been demon-possessed begged to go with him. Jesus did not let him, but said, "Go home to your own people and tell them how much the Lord has done for you, and how he has had mercy on you" (Mark 5:18-19), niv.

And the Lord said, "Simon, Simon! Indeed, Satan has asked for you, that he may sift you as wheat. But I have prayed for you, that your faith should not fail; and when you have returned to Me, strengthen your brethren" (Luke 22:31-32), lab.

And Jabez called on the God of Israel saying, "Oh, which you would bless me indeed, and enlarge my territory, that you would be with me, and that You would keep me for evil, that I may not cause pain !" So God granted him what he requested (I Chron. 4:10), nkjv.

And he said, A certain man had two sons: And the younger of them said to his father, "Father, give me the portion of goods that falls to me." And he divided to them his living. And not many days after, the younger son gathered all together, and he took his journey into a far county, and there he wasted his substance with riotous living."

Verse 17:
"But when he came to himself, he said, how many hired servants of my father's have bread enough and to spare, and I perish with hunger!"

Verse 21:
And the son said to him, Father, I have sinned against heaven and in your sight, and am no more worthy to be called your son."

Verse 24:
For this my son was dead and is alive again; he was lost and is found. And they began to be merry (Luke 15:11-13, 17, 21, 24), kjv.

How blessed is the man who endures temptation! When he has passed the test, he will receive the victor's crown of life that God has promised to those who keep on loving him, when someone is tempted, he should not say, "I am being tempted by God," because God cannot be tempted by evil, nor does he tempt anyone. Instead, each person is tempted by his own desire, being lured and trapped by it. Then, after desire has conceived, it gives birth to sin; and sin, when it is full-grown, gives birth to death. Don't be deceived, my dear brothers and sisters (Jam. 1:12-16), isv.

What do you think? If a man own a hundred sheep, and one of them wanders away, will he not leave the ninety-nine on the hills and go to look for the one that wandered off ? (Matt. 18:12), niv.

Suppose one of you has a hundred sheep and loses one of them. Doesn't he leave the ninety-nine in the open county and go after the lost sheep until he finds it? And when he finds, he joyfully puts it on his shoulders and goes home. Then he calls his friends and neighbors together and says, "Rejoice with me, I have found my lost sheep" (Luke 15:4-6), niv.

And I give unto them eternal life; and they shall never perish, neither shall any man pluck them out of my hand (John 10:28), kjv.

Blessed and worthy of praise be the God and Father of our Lord Jesus Christ, who has blessed us with every spiritual blessing in the heavenly realms in Christ, just as He chose us in Christ before the foundation of the world, so that we would be holy and blameless in His sight. In love He predestined and lovingly planned for us to be adopted to Himself as His own children through Jesus Christ, in accordance with the kind intention and good pleasure of his will (Ephes. 1:3-5), amp.

And I will make of thee a great nation and I will bless the, and make thy name great; and thou shalt be a blessing (Gen. 12:2), kjv.

A man's gift makes room for him and brings him before great men (Pro. 18:16), nasb.

By having the eyes of your heart flooded with light, so that you can know and understand the hope to which He has called you, and how rich is His glorious inheritance in the saints. His set apart ones (Eph. 1:18), amp.

Then Ziba said to the king, "According to all that my lord the king commands his servant, so will your servant do." So Mephibosheth ate regularly at David's table, like one of the king's own son (II Samuel 9:11), nlt.

www.ingramcontent.com/pod-product-compliance
Lightning Source LLC
Chambersburg PA
CBHW060522100426
42743CB00009B/1410